GROWING UP
sew liberated

----

making handmade
clothes + projects for
your creative child

Meg McElwee

INTERWEAVE
interweave.com

Editor Katrina Loving

Technical Editors Rebecca Kemp-Brent
Bernie Kulisek

Art Director Liz Quan

Designer Pamela Norman

Photographer Joe Hancock

Illustrator Ann Swanson

Production Katherine Jackson

Interweave Press LLC
201 East Fourth Street
Loveland, CO 80537
interweave.com

Printed in China by Asia Pacific Offset Ltd.

Par ITeach
J
646.4
McE
Main

Library of Congress Cataloging-
in-Publication Data

McElwee, Meg.
Growing up sew liberated : making handmade clothes
and projects for your creative child / Meg McElwee.
p. cm. Includes bibliographical references and index.
ISBN 978-1-59668-162-0 (pbk.)
1. Children's clothing--Patterns. 2. Children's
paraphernalia. 3. Creative activities and seat work.
4. Sewing. I. Title.
TT640.M35 2010
646.4'06--dc22
2010040620

10 9 8 7 6 5 4 3 2 1

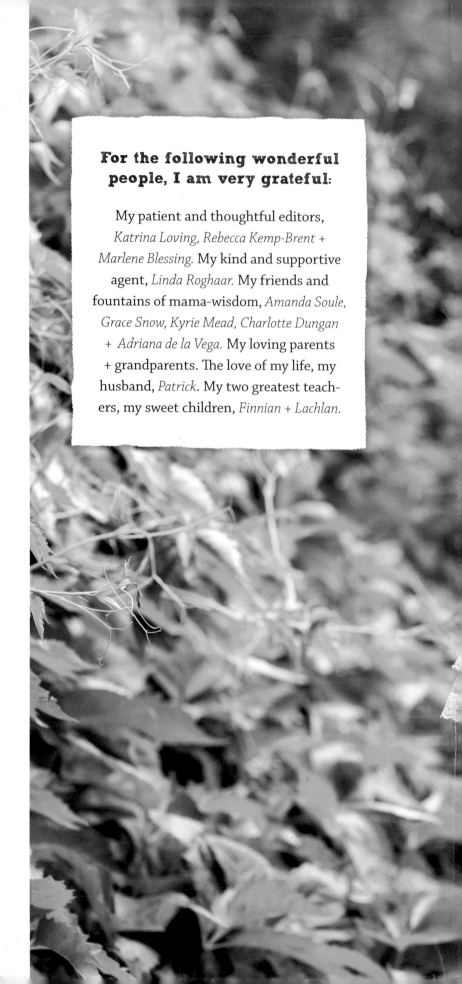

For the following wonderful people, I am very grateful:

My patient and thoughtful editors, *Katrina Loving, Rebecca Kemp-Brent + Marlene Blessing.* My kind and supportive agent, *Linda Roghaar.* My friends and fountains of mama-wisdom, *Amanda Soule, Grace Snow, Kyrie Mead, Charlotte Dungan + Adriana de la Vega.* My loving parents + grandparents. The love of my life, my husband, *Patrick.* My two greatest teachers, my sweet children, *Finnian + Lachlan.*

contents

Bringing *Handmade Beauty* Into Your Child's Life *Every* Day

Children move through their early years with a distinct rhythm—a keen awareness of the natural ebb and flow of seasons and days. While we adults are well aware of the abstract notion of clock-time, children have little interest in it. We have schedules to keep, appointments to attend, and multiple other demands on our time and energy. Children, on the other hand, have quite a different experience. From the newborn whose sleep cycle defies our own definitions of day and night to the three-year-old whose need for an afternoon nap is apparent without even a glance at a watch, young children live every day according to an organic, natural rhythm. As both a mom and an early childhood Montessori teacher, I have found that creating a routine for children relieves stress for the adults as well as the children. This perspective informed the creation of this book, which is full of sewing projects and activities specifically created with the daily activities of babies and young children in mind.

For me, sewing and other handwork (such as knitting) bring me to a place of peace-in-the-moment that recaptures that slow-moving, childlike sense of time. I had always felt this calming effect while in the midst of a sewing project, but since having my son, my creative time has become an anchor within the frenetic days of motherhood. Sewing can be such a balm for the busy soul, as long as you take the time to enjoy the process of creating and don't rush yourself to quickly churn out finished products. What is important is that your children see you enjoying your own creative process. It's also important for them to see you slow down, taking the time to do little things from hand embroidering a special apron to the way you gently sweep dollops of cookie dough from the spoon onto the cookie sheet.

Growing Up Sew Liberated is organized with the needs of the child and the family in mind. Young children thrive with a predictable routine as they move through their day. Certain touchstones, such as family meals, a daily walk, and evening baths can ease transitions and relieve anxiety. In this book, you'll find varied projects to incorporate into your daily routine with your child, along with ideas for games and routines for young children.

May your days with children be filled with creativity and joy.

Be pleasant
until ten o'clock
in the morning
and the rest of
the day will take
care of itself.

~ Elbert Hubbard,
American philosopher

greeting
the morning

Those words from Elbert Hubbard should be in a frame, displayed prominently above my kitchen table. Not prone to bubbly cheerfulness in the morning, I would benefit from this gentle reminder. In my experience, the words speak truth—a day is what you make of it, and the morning can make or break a day, especially when you have little ones afoot.

Morning time holds such optimism, such possibilities. The birds sing, the baby babbles, the seven-year-old tells you all about his dream, and you begin your day quietly, perhaps with a cup of tea or coffee in hand (especially if you have a baby who woke up several times during the night). We all have terrible, horrible, no good, very bad days on occasion—such is life. With a nod to the inevitable, we can focus on making most days start off smoothly and peacefully. A happy morning is the secret ingredient for a good day.

In our family, a good morning starts with the evening before. After our son is asleep, we go about preparing the home for the following morning. It's a nice way for my husband and me to spend twenty minutes together, enjoying adult conversation while busying our hands with little chores that will make the following morning just a bit easier.

The following pages contain comfy clothes that you can make for your little one. When the time comes to get dressed and start the day, your child will be clothed in a lovingly handmade item, such as the snuggly Heartwarming Reversible Baby Sweatshirt (page 12) or the sturdy-yet-adorable Basic Pocket Pants (page 30). The combination of a pleasant morning routine and the joy of seeing your own handiwork put to good use will get both you and your child off to a great start.

envelope
tees

I remember the rush of emotions as my new-born son squealed in protest during those first clothing changes. I soon opted for simple shirts to minimize time on the changing mat. Envelope Tees embody that simplicity, with classic unisex styling that makes them the perfect foundation for a child's wardrobe. They're easy to make and ripe with possibilities for personalization. Make them with short or long sleeves and add appliqués, lace, ruffles, or embroidery to match the personality of the wearer!

FINISHED SIZE 0–6 (6–12, 12–18, 18–24) months is 10 (10¾, 11¾, 12¼)" (25.5 [27.5, 30, 31] cm) long at center back. Refer to the Size Chart on page 145 for more fit information. Tee shown is size 0–6 months.

FABRIC + MATERIALS

☐ Short-sleeve tee: ½ (½, ⅝, ⅝) yd (46 [46, 57.5, 57.5] cm) of 60" (152.5 cm) wide cotton stretch knit (Main)

OR

Long-sleeve tee: ¾ (¾, ⅞, ⅞) yd (69 [69, 80, 80] cm) of 60" (152.5 cm) wide cotton stretch knit (Main)

☐ ⅛ yd (11.5 cm) of cotton rib knit (Contrast; all sizes)

☐ Coordinating sewing thread

☐ Swedish tracing paper or other pattern paper

TOOLS

☐ Envelope Tee pattern in pattern envelope

☐ Ballpoint or stretch sewing machine needle

☐ Fine ballpoint pins

☐ Rotary cutter, quilter's ruler, and self-healing mat (optional for cutting)

☐ Serger (optional)

notes

- ⅜" (1 cm) seam allowances are used unless otherwise noted.

- Remember to wash, dry, and press all fabric before beginning. Take care not to stretch the knit fabrics when pressing and cutting out the pieces.

- Make sure that the grainlines on the patterns run perpendicular to the stretchiest (usually crosswise) grain of the fabric.

- Refer to the Pattern Guide on page 146 for assistance with using the patterns; be sure to transfer all pattern markings to the fabric wrong side unless otherwise noted.

- See Working with Knits on page 139 for information about the best stitches for seams in knit fabrics.

- Be sure to use the ballpoint or stretch needle on your machine for the entire project, as you will be sewing on knit fabric.

Cut the Fabric

1 Trace the pattern pieces onto Swedish tracing paper or other pattern paper, transferring all pattern markings, and cut out. Refer to the layout diagrams on pages 147–148 for assistance with the following steps.

2 From the Main fabric, cut:
- * One Front on the fold
- * One Back on the fold
- * Two Sleeves (cut one, cut one reverse; use the Short Sleeve or the Long Sleeve, depending on your preference)

3 From the Contrast fabric, cut:
- * One Front Binding
- * One Back Binding

Sew on the Neck Bindings

4 Using a stretch or narrow zigzag stitch, sew one long edge of the Front Binding to the Front along the neck edge, right sides together. Gently stretch the Binding to fit as you sew **(fig. 01)**. Repeat to attach the Back Binding to the Back.

5 Press the Front Binding away from the Front. Using the iron's steam setting will help ease the pieces to fit without gathers. Turn the Binding raw edge to the wrong side, encircling the seam allowances, and press. The raw edge of the Binding will extend just below the seam on the wrong side of the Front. Pin the Binding in place. Repeat for the Back Binding.

6 From the right side of the Front, sew a zigzag stitch (2.0 mm wide and 2.0 mm long) along the bottom edge of the Binding, just above the previous seam. On the wrong side, the raw edge of the Binding will be caught in this seam, finishing the Binding. The unfinished ribbing on the wrong side won't ravel and will be less bulky and more comfortable against the skin than other finishes. Repeat entire step to finish the Back Binding.

Sew the Shoulders + Complete the Hems

7 Match the notches along the shoulders so that the Back overlaps the Front and match the bound edge of each piece to the dot on the other piece. Stretch the short ends of the bindings slightly so they will be entirely caught in the basting seam and pin the overlapped area in place. Sew zigzag basting seams a scant ⅛" (3 mm) from the raw edge of the shoulders, tacking down the overlapping shoulders **(fig. 02).**

8 If you have a serger, finish the bottom edges of the Front, Back, and Sleeves. If not, leave the fabric edges unfinished.

9 Press ¾" (2 cm) of the serged (or raw) edges toward the wrong side of the Front, Back, and Sleeves. Pin if desired; I find it easier to work without pins when stitching crosswise hems.

10 Use a zigzag or other stretch stitch to topstitch ⅝" (1.5 cm) from the folded edges of the hems.

Attach the Sleeves + Sew the Side Seams

11 Matching the notch on the Sleeve to the notch on the shoulder, pin the sleeve to the shoulder with right sides together and sew, using a ¼" (6 mm) seam allowance (**fig. 03**). Work with the sleeve on the bottom, allowing the feed dog to help ease the curves together. Repeat to attach the remaining sleeve to the other shoulder.

12 With the shirt inside out, align the side and underarm seams and pin in place. Sew one continuous ¼" (6 mm) seam, starting at the sleeve and continuing to the shirt's bottom hem (**fig. 04**). Repeat to finish the other side of the shirt. Press the seam allowances open if not serged.

13 To strengthen the seams, sew a few zigzag stitches (4.0 mm wide, 0.2 mm long) across the seam allowances at the shirt and sleeve hems.

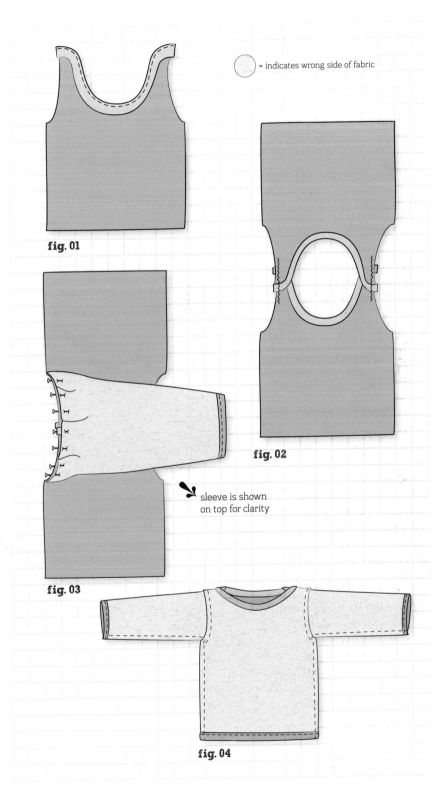

= indicates wrong side of fabric

fig. 01

fig. 02

fig. 03

sleeve is shown on top for clarity

fig. 04

heartwarming
reversible baby sweatshirt

Perfect for babies and toddlers, this cozy crossover sweatshirt is easy for a caregiver to put on and take off, and it is completely reversible, meaning that there are no scratchy exposed seams. Simply turn it inside out for a fresh, clean look if one side gets dirty. Pair it with the Reversible Bubble Pants (page 18) for an adorable and comfortable go-to outfit.

FINISHED SIZE 0–6 (6–12, 12–18, 18–24) months is 10 ¼ (11, 12, 12½)" (26 [28, 30.5, 31.5] cm) long at center back. Refer to the Size Chart on page 145 for more fit information. Sweatshirt shown is size 0–6 months.

FABRIC + MATERIALS

- ½ (½, ⅝, ⅝) yd (46 [46, 57.5, 57.5] cm) of 60" (152.5 cm) wide cotton interlock knit for shell (Main)

- ½ (½, ⅝, ⅝) yd (46 [46, 57.5, 57.5] cm) of 60" (152.5 cm) wide cotton interlock knit or cotton fleece for lining (Contrast)

- ⅛ yd (11.5 cm) of 60" (152.5 cm) wide cotton interlock knit or 1×1 lightweight rib knit for ties (all sizes)

- Coordinating sewing thread

- Swedish tracing paper or other pattern paper

- 1 small sew-on snap

TOOLS

- Baby Sweatshirt pattern in pattern envelope

- Ballpoint or stretch sewing machine needle

- Fine ballpoint pins

- Rotary cutter, quilter's ruler, and self-healing mat (optional for cutting)

- Walking foot for sewing machine (optional)

- Serger (optional)

notes

• ¼" (6 mm) seam allowances are used unless otherwise noted.

• Remember to wash, dry, and press all fabric before beginning. Take care not to stretch the knit fabrics when pressing and cutting out the pieces.

• See Working with Knits on page 139 for information about the best stitches for seams in knit fabrics.

• Refer to the Pattern Guide on page 146 for assistance with using the patterns; be sure to transfer all pattern markings to the fabric wrong side unless otherwise noted.

• Be sure to use the ballpoint or stretch needle on your machine for the entire project, as you will be sewing on knit fabric.

Cut the Fabric

1 Trace the pattern pieces onto Swedish tracing paper or other pattern paper, transferring all pattern markings, and cut out.

Fold the Main fabric in half lengthwise with right sides together. Cut the following pieces, referring to the layout diagram on page 149 for assistance:
  * One Back on the fold
  * Two Fronts
  * Two Sleeves

With the fabric folded, you will be cutting both Fronts and Sleeves at once, with one of each pair reversed. Repeat entire step to cut the Contrast fabric pieces for the lining.

2 From the tie fabric, cut two strips 1¾" × 14" (4.5 × 35.5 cm), with the long edge of each strip parallel to the stretchiest (usually crosswise) grain of the fabric.

Assemble the Shell + Lining

3 Begin with the Main fabric pieces. With right sides together, pin the Back to one Front at the shoulder, aligning the raw edges. Serge, mock overlock, or zigzag the shoulder seam and press both seam allowances toward the Back. Repeat to sew the second Front to the remaining shoulder seam.

4 With right sides together, align the center notch of one sleeve with one shoulder seam and pin. Continue to pin the sleeve to the bodice, matching the armhole and underarm raw edges. Sew along the armhole curve as shown in **fig. 01** and then press both seam allowances toward the sleeve. Work with the sleeve on the bottom, allowing the feed dogs to help ease the curves together. Repeat to join the remaining sleeve to the other armhole.

5 Pin the underarm and side seam edges together, matching the armhole seams, with right sides together. Sew from the sleeve hem to the garment hem in one continuous operation, taking care not to catch the edge of the opposite bodice under the needle as you sew (**fig. 02**). Press both seam allowances toward the back. Press ½" (1.3 cm) to the wrong side at the bottom of each sleeve.

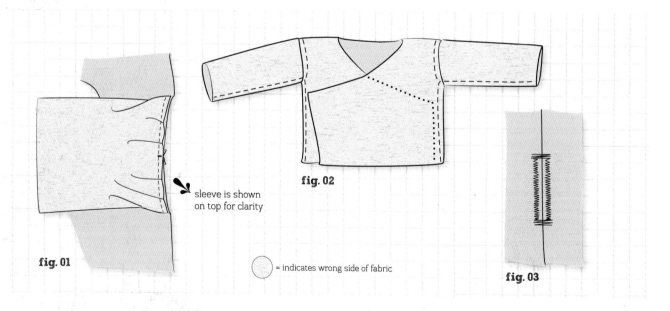

sleeve is shown on top for clarity

fig. 02

= indicates wrong side of fabric

fig. 01

fig. 03

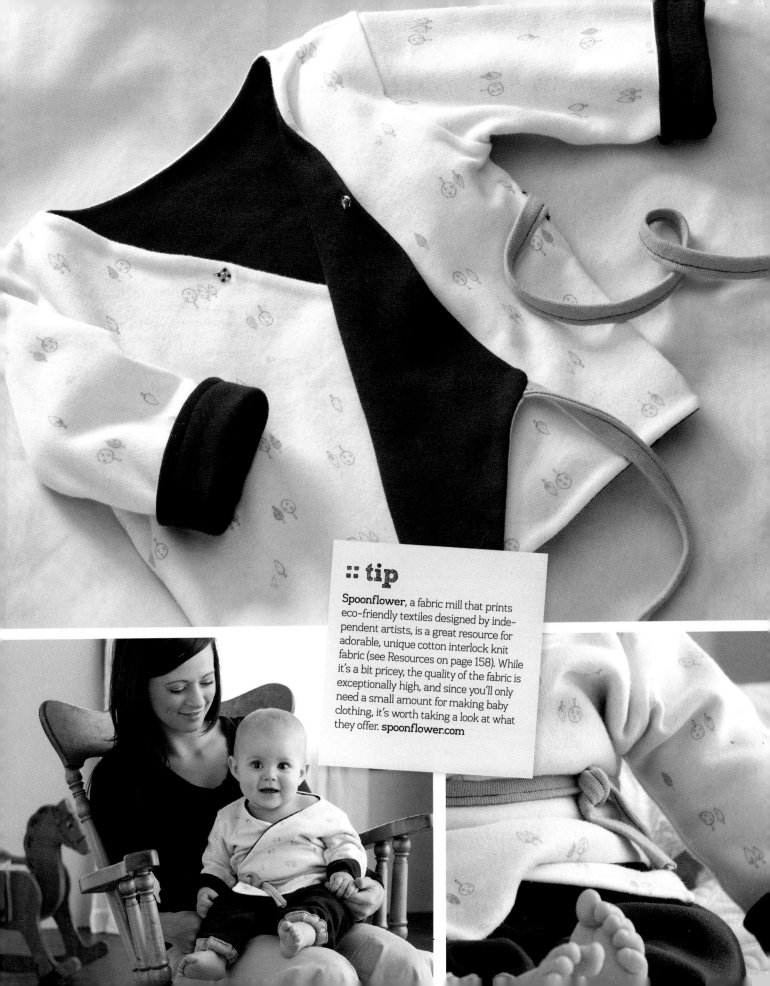

:: tip

Spoonflower, a fabric mill that prints eco-friendly textiles designed by independent artists, is a great resource for adorable, unique cotton interlock knit fabric (see Resources on page 158). While it's a bit pricey, the quality of the fabric is exceptionally high, and since you'll only need a small amount for making baby clothing, it's worth taking a look at what they offer. **spoonflower.com**

6 Repeat Steps 3–5 to assemble the Contrast fabric shirt for the lining, but reverse the pressing directions so the seams will nest together for less bulk in the finished garment. Press the shoulder and underarm/side seam allowances toward the front and press the armhole seam allowances toward the bodice.

Make the Ties

7 Create double-fold binding with each Tie strip, following the instructions under Double-Fold Binding on page 144, but fold the binding evenly, instead of slightly unevenly as instructed. Unfold one binding strip along the center crease, fold ½" (1.3 cm) toward the wrong side along one short edge, and press. Refold the strip along the existing center crease, enclosing the raw edges, and press again. The raw edges of one short end will remain exposed.

8 Use a walking foot, if available. To keep the fabric from being pushed into the needle hole, begin sewing ½" (1.3 cm) from the unfinished raw edge of the binding. Using a stretch stitch so that the stitching will not break when the tie is stretched, edgestitch (page 142) down the long doubled edge to close the binding, creating a tie. Cut away the unstitched ½" (1.3 cm) at the tie's raw edge. Repeat Steps 7 and 8 to make the second tie.

Set the Lining into the Shell

9 Turn the shell shirt (Main fabric) right side out. Keep the lining shirt (Contrast fabric) inside out. Lay the lining on a flat surface and insert the shell shirt sleeves into the lining sleeves, right sides together. Carefully arrange the shell so that it is completely tucked inside the lining, matching seams and edges. No part of

the shell right side should be peeking out from behind the lining wrong side. Pin together.

10 Insert one tie (made in Steps 7–8) into each side of the bodice at the front corners. Pin the unfinished short end of the tie ¼" (6 mm) below the front bodice corner, matching the raw edges, with the ties sandwiched between the shell and lining. The bulk of the tie will lie between the Main shirt and Lining; make sure that the ties are out of the way of the needle when you are sewing the seams. Repeat to attach the second tie to the other bodice.

11 Sew or serge the shell to the lining along the entire continuous unfinished edge of the shirt, catching the ends of the ties in the seam.

12 Reach into one of the sleeves and turn the garment right side out through the sleeve. Tuck the lining's sleeves back inside the shell sleeves and press the front/neckline/hem seam flat, with the ties extending from the corners of the right and left bodice fronts.

Finish the Sweatshirt

13 Smooth the shell fabric sleeve over the lining sleeve and align the underarm seams. Align and pin the folded edges. Topstitch (page 142) with a 3 mm straight stitch, ¼" (6 mm) from the pressed sleeve edges. Repeat entire step to finish the remaining sleeve.

14 Transfer the buttonhole placement from the pattern to the right side seam of the shirt, marking directly on top of the seamline. Use a removable marking tool, as the mark will be on the fabric right side.

15 Make sure that the lining and shell seams are aligned, one directly on top of the other, at the buttonhole mark. Secure the seams with pins or basting stitches outside the buttonhole area to keep the fabric from shifting. Refer to your machine's manual for specific instructions on making a buttonhole; many machines have automatic buttonholing features. If your machine doesn't have an automatic feature, make a buttonhole by stitching a tight zigzag stitch (.5 mm long × 2 mm wide) on either side of the seam, between the ends of the buttonhole mark. At each end of the buttonhole, widen the zigzag stitch to 5 mm, reduce the length to 0.3 mm, and make several securing stitches, joining the ends of the two lines of stitching (**fig. 03** on page 14).

16 Use a seam ripper or embroidery scissors to cut through the seam/center of the buttonhole, being careful not to cut through any of the buttonhole stitches.

17 Mark the placement of the snap components where the right and left front bodices cross at the neckline by making a dot with a fabric pen on the inside of the overlapping bodice piece and a corresponding mark on the exterior of the underlying piece.

18 Thread a handsewing needle and use a whipstitch (page 143) to attach the female snap component to the underlying bodice, directly on top of the mark. Sew the male snap component to the inside of the overlapping piece, at the mark. Thread the tie from the underlapping side of the sweatshirt front through the buttonhole to tie the sweatshirt.

thoughts on children's clothing

Clothing acts as our second skin, protecting us from the elements and providing warmth. As adults, the clothing we choose might identify us as members of a group or profession, signal an important occasion, or it might be a tool with which to express ourselves socially. For children, the considerations to take into account when choosing clothing are a bit different. As a mother (and therefore frequent decision-maker on my young son's clothing), I ask myself three questions when making or purchasing clothing for little ones:

Is it comfortable?

• Babies and young children should always be dressed in comfortable clothes. They are just learning about the world, and we want to surround them with positive impressions of it. My preference is for organic cotton and wool knit fabrics. In a warm climate, I love making shirts and pants out of woven linen/cotton blends. I avoid synthetic fibers, as they don't breathe as well as natural fibers.

Here are some things to consider, in terms of comfort, when choosing fabrics or buying ready-made clothing:

• Pay attention to how a fabric feels against the skin and remember that young children have more sensitive skin than most adults. Go with the highest quality fabrics that fit your budget.

• Take a look at the seams on the inside of the garment. Are they exposed? Do they feel rough? Newborns especially should be dressed in clothing without exposed seams. Their clothing should be lined or worn inside-out with the seams facing out and the softer side next to their skin. Both babies and older children often prefer knit clothing that has flatlocked seams that lie flat due to the construction method.

Does it allow free movement?

• This question pertains to little girls, especially. Boy's clothing seems designed for ease of movement, but for some reason, that's not always the case for girls. Children of both genders need to be free to move their bodies, to climb, to explore, and to get dirty outside. While there is certainly a time for dressing up for special occasions, this should be kept to a minimum, for little ones especially. For example, a crawling baby girl shouldn't wear dresses or longer tunic tops, as they will impede her ability to crawl. If you have an older girly-girl, try to find her some comfortable knit dresses (hannaandersson.com has a good selection) that can be worn with leggings or shorts underneath so her play won't be affected by her wardrobe.

• In general, I prefer stretchy knit fabrics for babies and young children, as they move with the body and are not constricting. Cotton interlock is perfect for pants—fortunately, knit pants are easy to whip up even if you don't have a serger. If you've never worked with knit fabrics before, you have nothing to fear! Check out Working with Knits on page 139 before diving into your first knitwear project. I've focused mostly on knitwear in this book because, while there are plenty of children's patterns intended for use with woven fabrics, good knit patterns are harder to find.

Does it promote independence?

• This is a big one—a key to avoiding frustration and meltdowns in young children (and keeping mom or dad sane). Children tend to prefer clothing that they can put on and take off themselves! Jeans are a big culprit here—a three year-old may not be able to undo a belt, a metal button, and a zipper and still make it to the bathroom in time. The same goes for overalls. If your child is becoming toilet independent, then they'll definitely need to easily get in and out of clothes for this purpose. Look for elastic waistbands, large toggles, or button closures instead of zippers. A good time for kids to practice with new closures is in doll play (see the Little Amigo Cloth Doll on page 56) or while playing dress up (see the Dress-Up Bucket on page 76). Of course, babies are different, as they aren't dressing themselves, but the same principles will then apply to you—if you can't get it on and off your wiggly baby without frustration, then it's probably too complicated for him or her to be wearing!

• When you find a particular style that works for your child, sew up or purchase several garments in that style to make the choice of outfits easier. Some young children enjoy choosing their outfits, some children find this difficult, and some children couldn't care less what they wear! The choice, however, should be very simple, such as the choice between a red shirt and a white shirt of the same style. Try storing the majority of your young child's clothes in another room (instead of their own room), pulling out two appropriate choices for the day, and letting your child choose between them.

reversible
bubble pants

These pants are a necessity for babies who wear bulky cloth diapers, and you'll find that disposable-diaper wearers will enjoy the freedom of movement as well. My son, who wore cloth diapers, reached

a point where even typical store-bought knit pants were too tight on him and his movement was restricted. And so, the Bubble Pants were born—roomy pants designed to allow maximum unrestricted movement for sitters, crawlers, and beyond. The cuffs are finished with elastic to keep the fabric from extending beyond the ankle and getting in the way of babies on the move.

FINISHED SIZE Pants fit 0–6 (6–12, 12–18, 18–24) months with a 6 (7½, 8½, 10)" (15 [19, 21.5, 25.5] cm) inseam. Refer to the Size Chart on page 145 for more fit information. Pants shown are size 6–12 months.

FABRIC + MATERIALS

- ⬧ ⅔ (⅔, ¾, ¾) yd (57.5 [57.5, 69, 69] cm) of 60" (152.5 cm) wide cotton interlock knit for shell (Main)

- ⬧ ⅔ (⅔, ¾, ¾) yd (57.5 [57.5, 69, 69] cm) of 60" (152.5 cm) wide cotton interlock knit in a second color for lining (Contrast)

- ⬧ 30 (31½, 32¾, 34)" (76 [80, 83, 86.5] cm) length of ¼" (6 mm) wide elastic

- ⬧ Coordinating sewing thread

- ⬧ Swedish tracing paper or other pattern paper

TOOLS

- ⬧ Bubble Pants pattern in pattern envelope

- ⬧ Ballpoint or stretch sewing machine needle

- ⬧ Fine ballpoint pins

- ⬧ Rotary cutter, quilting ruler, and self-healing mat (optional for cutting)

- ⬧ Walking foot for sewing machine (optional)

- ⬧ Safety pin

- ⬧ Serger (optional)

notes

- ¼" (6 mm) seam allowances are used unless otherwise noted.

- Remember to wash, dry, and press all fabric before beginning. Take care not to stretch the knit fabrics when pressing and cutting out the pieces.

- See Working with Knits on page 139 for information about the best stitches for seams in knit fabrics.

- Be sure to use the ballpoint or stretch needle on your machine for the entire project, as you will be sewing on knit fabric.

- Refer to the Pattern Guide on page 146 for assistance with using the patterns; be sure to transfer all pattern markings to the fabric wrong side unless otherwise noted.

- If you are using a directional print, make sure all pattern pieces are oriented appropriately before cutting.

- Woven cotton or cotton flannel can be substituted for the knit fabrics used here. If you decide to make a pair of Bubble Pants from a woven fabric, be sure you have the appropriate sewing machine needle for your fabric selection (consult your sewing machine manual). It may also be necessary to choose a larger size for the garment without the stretch of a knit fabric.

Trace Pattern + Cut Fabric

1 Trace the pattern pieces onto Swedish tracing paper or other pattern paper, transferring all pattern markings, and cut out. Note that there are separate cutting lines for the Shell and Lining legs.

2 Cut the following pieces from the Main fabric, referring to the layout

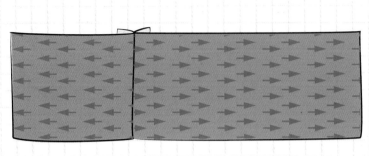

fig. 01

diagram on page 149 for assistance, and transferring the pattern markings to the wrong side of the fabric:

    * Two Pant Legs
    * One Front Gusset
    * One Back Gusset

Repeat to cut the following pieces from the Contrast fabric:

    * Two Pant Leg Linings
    * One Front Gusset
    * One Back Gusset

Assemble the Pants

3 Begin with the Main fabric pieces. Fold one of the Pant Legs in half lengthwise with right sides together, matching the lower notches, and pin together along the inside of the leg. Sew from the bottom raw edge to the lower notch. Press the seam open. Repeat entire step with the second Pant Leg, then repeat again to assemble the lining Pant Legs.

4 Take the Main fabric Front and Back Gussets and place them right sides together, matching the notches on the short edges. Pin and sew along the notched short edge; press the seam open. If the fabric is directional, the

prints should be mirror images of each other, as shown in **fig. 01**. Repeat entire step to assemble the Contrast fabric gusset.

5 Pin one Main fabric Pant Leg to the Main fabric Gusset, right sides together, matching the seams and notches (**fig. 02** on page 22). Sew and press the seam open. Pin the second Main fabric Pant Leg to the free side of the Gusset as before. Sew and press the seam open. Repeat entire step to sew the Contrast Pant Legs to the Contrast Gusset. You have now assembled the shell pants and lining pants.

6 Turn the shell pants (Main fabric) right side out and the lining pants (Contrast fabric) wrong side out. Slip the shell pants inside the lining pants, right sides together, and align the waist edges. Match the Gusset/Pant Leg seams and pin the pants along the waist. Sew the entire waist edge. Turn the pants right side out through one of the leg openings, then tuck the Contrast pants inside the Main pants, aligning the seams so the legs are not twisted. All seam allowances will be hidden between the layers.

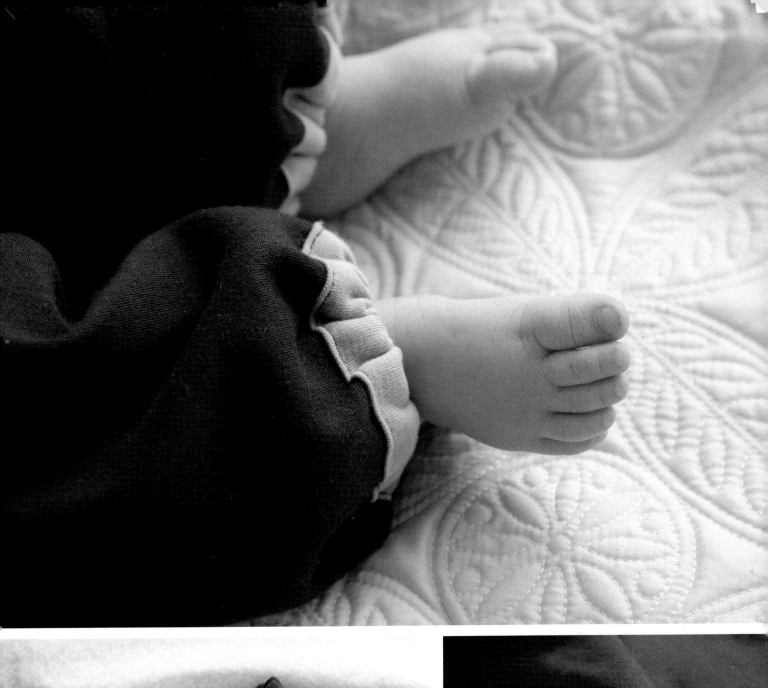

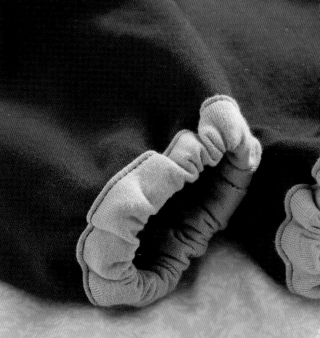

Make the Elastic Casing

7 Press the waist edge flat. Topstitch (page 142) ⅝" (1.5 cm) from the waist edge, leaving a 1" (2.5 cm) opening at the center back, to form the elastic casing.

8 Attach a safety pin to one end of a 17 (17½, 18, 18⅜)" (43 [44.5, 45.5, 46.8] cm) length of the ½" (1.3 cm) wide elastic, then insert the safety pin into the casing through the opening left in Step 7. Pin the tail end of the elastic to the pants to keep it from being pulled into the casing. Use the safety pin at the leading edge to work the elastic through the casing, working it along from the outside with your fingers, until it returns to the opening. Remove the safety pins and distribute the fabric evenly along the elastic, adjusting the length of the elastic for a tighter fit if desired. Be sure the elastic remains untwisted. Overlap the ends of the elastic ½" (1.3 cm) and fasten securely by stitching back and forth a few times through both layers (**fig. 03**). Guide the join of the elastic into the casing until it is hidden.

9 Topstitch ⅝" (1.5 cm) from the waistline to close the gap and complete the casing stitches.

Make the Cuff Casings to Finish

10 The lining fabric extends 1¼" (3.2 cm) beyond the shell at each leg opening. Press ¼" (6 mm) to the wrong side of each lining pant leg, then fold and press an additional 1" (2.5 cm) to the wrong side. Fold the lining fabric over the shell fabric, tucking the shell fabric raw edge into the lining fold so the lining is visible on the pants right side, and pin. With a 3.0 mm straight stitch, edgestitch (page 142) along the upper fold, leaving a 1" (2.5 cm) gap at the inseam, creating a casing for the elastic.

11 Cut two 6½ (7, 7⅜, 7¾)" (16.5 [18, 18.8, 19.5] cm) lengths of elastic. Repeat Step 8 to insert the elastic into each cuff casing and secure the elastic. Sew the casing gap closed, completing the edgestitching along the lining fold.

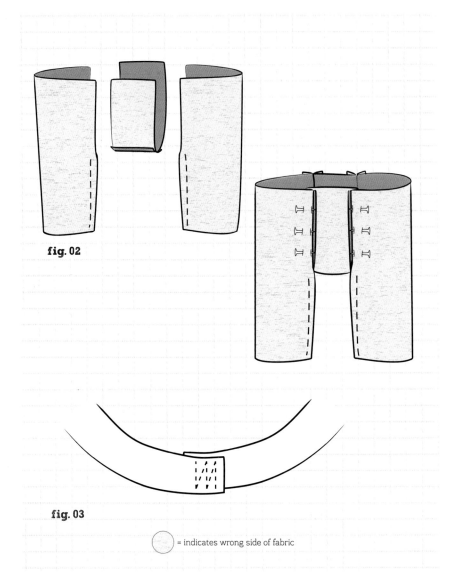

fig. 02

fig. 03

⊘ = indicates wrong side of fabric

tiny baby leggings

These mini leg warmers not only make for easier diaper changes, but they also keep your sweet babe's legs warm *during* the change. An Envelope Tee and a pair of these Leggings are perfect to throw on with a diaper so your little one can crawl or toddle around the house on a lazy day. You'll make your own pattern according to your baby's leg measurements; this will give you the best fit for your baby.

FINISHED SIZE Varies with measurements for a custom fit.

FABRIC + MATERIALS
- ¼–⅜ yd (23–34.5 cm) 45" (114.5 cm) wide light-weight ribbed knit cotton
- Coordinating sewing thread

TOOLS
- Ballpoint or stretch sewing machine needle
- Handsewing needle
- Fine, ballpoint pins

notes

- ¼" (6 mm) seam allowances are used unless otherwise noted.

- Refer to all other Notes on page 20.

- It can be tricky to get the presser foot to sew along such a tight tube. I find it helps to sew from the inside of the tube, inserting the presser foot into the tube, with its right edge parallel to the raw edges of the tube opening. The fabric will curl around above the foot, rather than bunching up underneath the fabric and foot as it would if you were sewing from the outside of the tube (see **fig. 01** on page 120 for assistance).

1 Measure the baby's leg around the upper thigh. Because the fabric is stretchy, this measurement will be used as the pattern width, with no ease or seam allowances added.

2 Measure the baby's leg from the upper thigh to the ankle. Add ½" (1.3 cm) for seam allowances and use the result as the pattern length.

3 Cut four rectangles the length and width determined above. Be sure the width measurement lies on the crosswise grain, where the fabric stretch is greatest.

4 Fold one of the rectangles in half lengthwise, matching the long edges. Sew the long edge, forming a tube. Press the seam allowances open. Repeat for the other three rectangles.

5 Turn one tube right side out so that the seam allowances are hidden inside. Insert this tube into a second tube that is wrong side out (the seam allowances are on the outside). Position the seam allowances opposite each other to reduce bulk. Align the short raw edges of the tubes and pin. Sew around the tube at one end, adjusting the machine for a wider stitch (2.0–2.5 mm), if desired.

6 Turn the outer tube right side out, beginning from the open end, forming a long tube with no visible seam allowances. Press the seam allowance to the wrong side on both unfinished edges. Tuck one tube inside the other, forming a fully lined tube. Pin the pressed edges together, then use a stretch stitch or 2.0–2.5 mm wide zigzag stitch to sew around the short edge of the tube through all layers, stretching the fabric slightly as you sew. This stitching will be visible on the outside of the leggings.

crossover tees

Here's a versatile unisex shirt for toddlers and "big kids" that can be made with either short or long sleeves and has great layering possibilities. This tee is quick to make, once you get the hang of it! The look can be more stylized for a girl by stretching out the ribbing on the short-sleeved version to create a slightly puffed cap sleeve (see page 141 for instructions). This simple style also lends itself to embellishment, such as adding a photo patch of the family pet (see page 29 for instructions). Have the recipient choose favorite colors for the tee, then complete a cute outfit by pairing the tee with the Basic Pocket Pants (page 30) for daytime or the Sleeping Johns (page 118) for a great pajama set.

FINISHED SIZE 2T (3T, 4T, 5) is 15¼ (16, 16½, 17)" (38.5 [40.5, 42, 43] cm) long at center back. Refer to the Size Chart on page 145 for more fit information. Tee shown is a size 3T.

FABRIC + MATERIALS

◻ Short-sleeve tee: ⅝ (⅝, ¾, ¾) yd (57.5 [57.5, 69, 69] cm) of 60" (152.5 cm) wide cotton jersey or interlock knit (Main) or Long-sleeve tee: ⅝ (⅝, ¾, ¾) yd (57.5 [57.5, 69, 69] cm) of 60" (152.5 cm) wide cotton jersey or interlock knit (Main)

◻ ⅛ yd (11.5 cm) of 45–60" (114.5–152.5 cm) wide lightweight 1×1 rib knit or cotton interlock knit for contrast ribbing (all sizes)

◻ Coordinating sewing thread

◻ Swedish tracing paper or other pattern paper

TOOLS

◻ Crossover Tee pattern in pattern envelope

◻ Ballpoint or stretch sewing machine needle

◻ Fine ballpoint pins

◻ Rotary cutter, quilter's ruler, and self-healing mat (optional for cutting)

◻ Walking foot for sewing machine (optional)

◻ Handsewing needle

◻ Serger (optional; see Notes)

notes

- ¼" (1 cm) seam allowances are used unless otherwise noted.

- Remember to wash, dry, and press all fabric before beginning. Take care not to stretch the knit fabrics when pressing and cutting out the pieces.

- See Working with Knits on page 139 for information about the best stitches for seams in knit fabrics.

- Refer to the Pattern Guide on page 146 for assistance with using the patterns; be sure to transfer all pattern markings to the fabric wrong side unless otherwise noted.

- Be sure to use the ballpoint or stretch needle on your machine for the entire project, as you will be sewing on knit fabric.

- If you use a serger, use wooly nylon thread in the bottom loopers for a less scratchy seam finish.

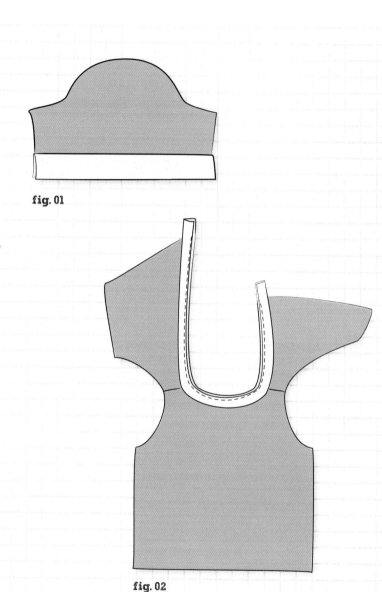

fig. 01

fig. 02

Cut the Fabric

1 Trace the pattern pieces onto Swedish tracing paper or other pattern paper, transferring all pattern markings, and cut out.

2 From the Main fabric, cut the following pieces as directed, referring to the layout diagram on page 150 for assistance:
- ✷ One Back on the fold
- ✷ One Left Front Overlap Bodice
- ✷ One Right Front Underlap Bodice (in the instructions, bodice pieces are referred to simply as "Left Bodice" and "Right Bodice" or "Bodices")
- ✷ Two Sleeves (either the long or short sleeve, depending on your desired style)

3 From the ribbing, cut the following pieces with the ribs perpendicular to the long edge and the greatest stretch running parallel to the long edge:
- ✷ Two strips 36" long × 2" wide (91.5 × 5 cm)

:: tip

It can sometimes be difficult to tell the right from the wrong side when using a knit fabric. It helps to make a mark on the wrong side of the cut pieces with a water-soluble fabric pen, tailor's chalk, or a piece of masking tape.

For a short-sleeved shirt:
   * Two strips, each 14" × 2"
   (35.5 × 5 cm)
For a long-sleeved shirt:
   * Two strips, each 10" × 4"
   (25.5 × 10 cm)

Attach the Ribbing to the Sleeves

4 Prepare all ribbing pieces (cut in Step 3) by folding each in half lengthwise, with wrong sides together, matching the raw edges. Press the fold, being careful not to stretch the ribbing. Set aside the longer strips.

5 Prepare the sleeve ribbings as instructed on page 141. Pin one strip to one sleeve's lower edge, right sides together, matching the raw edges (**fig. 01**). Sew together along the edge, feeding the sleeve and ribbing under the presser foot steadily and evenly without stretching. I find it easier to work without pins when you are attaching the ribbing.

For a puff sleeve, prepare the ribbing as directed above, then trim 2" (5 cm) from the length of each strip. Pin the ribbing to the sleeve at both underarm seams and at the center, then stretch the ribbing to fit as you sew. When the ribbing relaxes, it will gently gather the sleeve, making it puff. Press the seam allowances away from the ribbing. Repeat the entire step to finish the edge of the remaining sleeve.

Assemble the Tee

6 Pin the Back to the Bodice pieces at the shoulders, right sides together, taking care to keep the Left and Right Bodices in the correct positions. Serge, overcast, or stretch stitch both shoulder seams, and press toward the back.

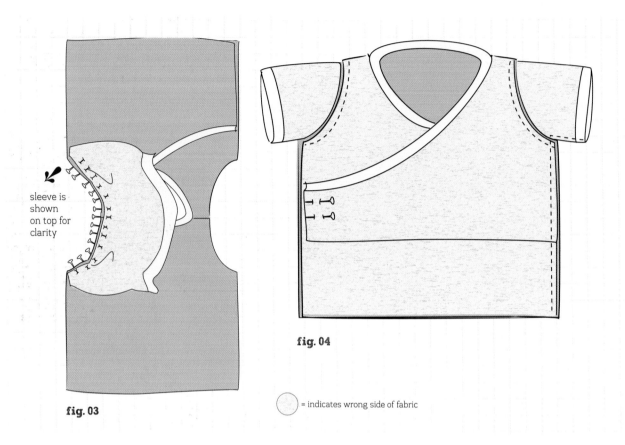

sleeve is
shown
on top for
clarity

fig. 03

fig. 04

◯ = indicates wrong side of fabric

7 Sew one of the long strips of folded ribbing along the neck edge, leaving at least a 1" (2.5 cm) tail of ribbing beyond each edge of the shirt. The long unfinished edges of the ribbing should align with the raw neck edge, as in Step 5. With the shirt lying flat (see **fig. 02** on page 26), start sewing at the side edge of the Right Bodice. Continue up and over the shoulder seam, along the back neck, over the left shoulder seam, and to the side edge of the Left Bodice (**fig. 02** on page 26). Pull gently at the ribbing as you sew, just enough to ease (page 142) the ribbing onto the edge without causing puckers in the shirt fabric. Press the seam allowances away from the ribbing.

8 With right sides together, align the center notch of one sleeve cap (upper curve) with the shoulder seam on one side. Working with the sleeve on the bottom, pin in place. Continue to pin the sleeve to the bodice, raw edges matched, easing the fabrics around the curves. Sew along the curve and then press the seam allowances toward the sleeve (**fig. 03**). Repeat to join the remaining sleeve to the other armhole.

Sew the Bodice + the Right Underarm/Side Seam

9 Arrange the shirt as it will appear when finished, wrong sides together, matching the raw edges at the side and underarm seams. The ribbing ends will extend past the side seams.

Tuck the Right Bodice under the Left Bodice as shown in the photographs. Align the Bodice side seams, matching the notches on the right side seam and positioning the Right Bodice between the notches on the left side seam, and pin the front bodices together; do not pin the Back to the fronts. Smooth the Bodices across the front and pin them together where the neckline edges cross, taking care not to pin through the Back.

10 Set the machine for a 3.0 mm straight stitch. Unfold the shirt and edgestitch (page 142) on the garment fabric a scant ⅛" (3 mm) from the ribbing, beginning on the overlapping Bodice at the right side seam and sewing through both Bodices. Con-

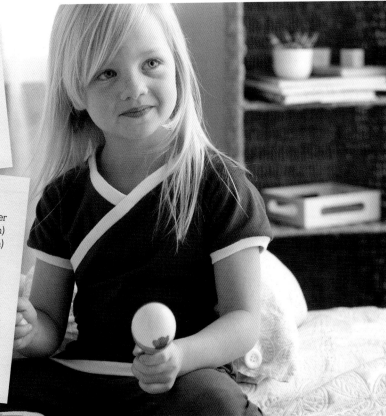

tinue edgestitching in one continuous
line, following the ribbing, over the
shoulder, around the back neck, and
down the underlapping Bodice. Fold
the ribbing on the Left Bodice out of
the way and complete the edgestitching under the ribbing where the two
seamlines cross. You've secured the
neck seam allowance with a line of
edgestitching. If you prefer, simply
stitch in the ditch (page 142) from the
right side seam to the crossover point.

11 Pin the assembled front to the
Back along the right side seam,
right sides together, continuing to pin
the sleeve underarm seam. Begin at the
sleeve edge and sew in one continuous
seam all the way to the bottom of the

shirt, making sure to catch the end of
the ribbing in the seam (**fig. 04**). Trim
any excess ribbing that extends beyond
the seam allowances and press the
seam allowances toward the back.

Attach the Bottom Ribbing + Sew the Left Side Seam

12 With the shirt still inside out,
align the left side of the shirt as
you did the right side and pin the left
side seam, leaving the last 4" (10 cm)
open.

13 Prepare the remaining long,
folded strip of ribbing as
instructed on page 141 and pin it to
the unfinished bottom edge of the
shirt, right sides together and raw

edges matched. The ribbing should be
the same length as the garment edge,
unless a puffy sweatshirt-type hem is
desired. Sew the ribbing to the shirt
and press the seam allowances away
from the ribbing.

14 Finish pinning the left side
seam. Sew and press the
underarm/side seam as in Step 11.

basic

pocket pants

When you're a child, there's always something interesting to pick up and put in a pocket for safekeeping, so pockets are a must. These sturdy pants are cute as well as practical. Contrast cuffs and binding add some nice detail, while the simple construction offers the opportunity to add your own personal touch with a bit of embroidery around the cuff or a patch on one knee. Although the pants featured here are made from soft denim, many other woven fabrics would work nicely. Try a printed denim, sturdy cotton, linen, or corduroy. It's all up to you!

FINISHED SIZE 2T (3T, 4T, 5) is 18 (20⅛, 22⅜, 24½)" (45.5 [51, 56, 62] cm) long at the side seam. Refer to the Size Chart on page 145 for more fit information. Pants shown are a size 3T.

FABRIC + MATERIALS

- ⅔ (⅔, ⅞, ⅞) yd (61 [61, 80, 80] cm) of 45" (114.5 cm) wide OR ⅔ (⅔, ¾, ¾) yd (61 [61, 69, 69] cm) of 60" (152.5 cm) wide solid color soft denim, twill, corduroy, or soft cotton (Main)

- ½ yd (46 cm) of 45–60" (114.5–152.5 cm) wide cotton fabric for cuffs, binding, and casing (Contrast; see notes)

23½ (24½, 25½, 26½)" (60 [62.5, 65, 67.5] cm) of ¾" (2 cm) wide elastic for waistband

- Coordinating sewing thread

- Swedish tracing paper or other pattern paper

TOOLS

- Basic Pocket Pants pattern in pattern envelope

- Rotary cutter, quilter's ruler, and self-healing mat (optional for cutting)

- Safety pin

- Walking foot (optional)

- Serger (optional)

notes

- All seam allowances are ½" (1.3 cm) unless otherwise indicated.
- Remember to wash, dry, and press all fabrics before sewing.
- For the pants shown, the wrong side of the Main fabric was used as the Contrast fabric.
- Use the Itch-Free Finish for exposed seams (see the sidebar on page 35).

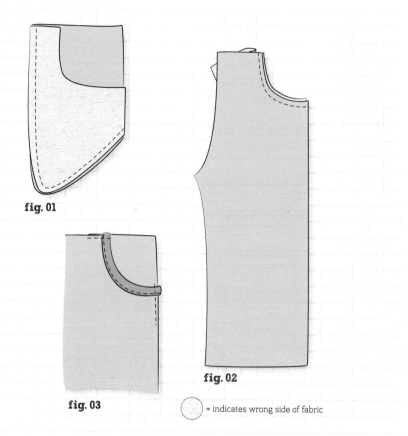

fig. 01

fig. 03

fig. 02

⊘ = indicates wrong side of fabric

Cut + Prepare the Fabric

1 Trace the patterns onto Swedish tracing paper or other pattern paper, transferring all pattern markings, and cut out. Fold the Main fabric in half lengthwise with right sides together and cut the following pieces, referring to the layout diagrams on pages 151–153 for assistance. The fabric is doubled, so you'll be cutting both pieces at the same time.

- ∗ Two Backs
- ∗ Two Fronts
- ∗ Two Pocket Backs
- ∗ Two Pocket Fronts

2 From the Contrast fabric, cut the following pieces as directed:

- ∗ Two Cuffs
- ∗ One Casing
- ∗ One Pocket Binding on the bias

3 To prepare for using the "Itch-Free" finishing method (see the sidebar on page 35), zigzag or serge all the edges of both pant Front and Back pieces.

Prepare the Pockets

4 Follow the instructions under Double-Fold Binding on page 144 to make ½" (1.3 cm) wide double-fold bias binding from the Pocket Binding piece. This will be used to accent (and finish) the top edges of the two pockets. If you are using the denim wrong side as the Contrast, remember to make the binding with the wrong side out.

5 Pin a Pocket Back to the corresponding Pocket Front with right sides together. Pin and sew along the curved edge (**fig. 01**). Repeat entire step to prepare the second pocket.

6 Match one assembled pocket to the corresponding pant Front, with the Pocket Front's wrong side against the pant Front's wrong side. Align the curved raw edges of the pant and Pocket Fronts and pin together. Increase the stitch length to 3.0 mm and baste (page 142) ¼" (6 mm) from the curved edge as shown in **fig. 02**, folding the Pocket Back out of the way and catching only the pant and Pocket Fronts in the basting.

See Steps 1 and 2 of Attach Binding with Mitered Corners on page 144 for assistance with the following step.

7 Slip the binding over the curved basted edges, sliding the raw edges of the curve completely into the binding center crease. Be sure to place the slightly longer side of the binding on the inside of the pocket. Stretch the binding slightly to ease it around the curve and pin the binding in place. Reset the stitch length to 2.5 mm and edgestitch (page 142) along the binding's lower fold,

stitching through all layers, keeping the Pocket Back folded away from the seam. Check often to ensure that the binding on the inside of the pocket is also caught in the seam. Trim the binding even with the raw edges of the pant.

8 Increase the stitch length to 4.0 mm and baste the pocket and pant together ¼" (6 mm) from the waist and side edges, including the Pocket Back in the basting (**fig. 03**).

9 Repeat Steps 6–8 to attach the other pocket to the remaining pant Front, using the leftover Pocket Binding.

Assemble the Pants

10 Place the pant Fronts right sides together, matching the curved raw edges. Pin together and sew the curved crotch seam. Finish the seam using the "Itch-Free" method at right. Repeat to sew the pant Backs together at the crotch.

11 Pin the assembled front and back right sides together and sew the side seams. Finish the seams as before, catching the pocket and its binding in the finishing stitches. If necessary, switch to a larger needle to sew through the bulky pocket opening.

12 Sew the entire inseam, beginning at the bottom of one leg and sewing up the leg, across the crotch, and down to the other leg opening. Finishing this seam with the "Itch-Free" method can be a bit tricky once you get to Step d of the process. To finish the seams, keep the project inside out and begin sewing at the crotch, sewing each leg separately with the lines of stitching broken at the crotch. Sew slowly, keeping the bulk of the pants fabric away from the feed dogs and presser foot.

Make the Waistband Casing

If you are using the wrong side of denim fabric as the Contrast, remember to reverse right and wrong sides in the instructions so the finished Casing will contrast with the pants.

13 Fold the Casing in half width-wise, right sides together and raw edges matched. Sew along the short end. Press the seam open.

14 With the pants still inside out, pin one long edge of the casing to the raw edge of the pant waist, aligning the Casing seam with the center back seam of the pants and laying the Casing right side against the wrong side of the pants fabric. Sew around the entire pant waist (**fig. 04**), then trim the seam allowance to ⅛" (3 mm). Press the seam open.

15 Turn the pants right side out. Press ¼" (6 mm) to the wrong side along the Casing raw edge. Fold

the casing to the pants right side along the seamline and press. Pin the folded edge in place and then edgestitch the waistband along the fold, leaving a 2" (5 cm) opening at the center back for threading the elastic.

16 Attach a safety pin to one end of the elastic, then insert the safety pin into the casing through the opening. Pin the tail end of the elastic to the pants so that it won't be drawn into the casing. Use the leading safety pin (inside the casing) to work the elastic through the casing with your fingers until it returns to the opening. Remove the safety pin and distribute the fabric evenly along the elastic, adjusting the length of the elastic for a tighter or looser fit if desired; unpin the tail end of the elastic but ensure that it does not slip back into the casing. Overlap the ends of the elastic by about ½" (1.3 cm) and stitch together securely by stitching back and forth a few times in a zigzag pattern (**fig. 05**). Guide the

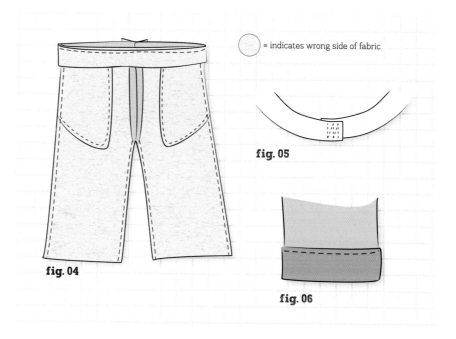

= indicates wrong side of fabric

fig. 04

fig. 05

fig. 06

join of the elastic into the casing until it is hidden. Edgestitch the opening in the casing closed, matching the previous stitch line.

Make the Cuffs + Finish the Pants

If you are using the wrong side of denim fabric as the Contrast, remember to seam the Cuffs with the wrong sides together so the finished Cuffs will contrast with the pants.

17 Fold one Cuff in half widthwise, right sides together, with the short ends aligned. Pin along the short edge and sew, forming a tube. Press the seam open. Repeat to make a tube with the remaining Cuff. Turn the tubes right side out.

18 Place one cuff tube inside the bottom of one pant leg, with the cuff right side against the pant leg's wrong side. Align the cuff tube seam with the pants inseam, match the pant and cuff raw edges, and pin in place. Sew the seam joining the cuff and pant leg.

19 Pull the cuff tube away from the pant leg and press the seam allowances toward the cuff. Press ½" (1.3 cm) to the wrong side along the cuff raw edge. Fold the cuff to the pants right side, around the seam allowances, so the cuff/pant seam is ½" (1.3 cm) above the fold and inside the pant leg. Press the fold at the bottom of the pant leg and then pin the folded cuff edge in place. Edgestitch the cuff's folded upper edge to the pants (**fig. 06**). As the child grows, lengthen the pants by rolling more of the cuff to the inside of the pant leg, restitching the fold so it lies lower on the pant leg, extending the life of the pants.

itch-free finish for exposed seams

In order to make finishing the seams easier, I find it helpful to prepare the edges before assembly by zigzagging or serging ⅛" (3 mm) from the raw edges. Be sure the edge finish does not compromise the accuracy of the seam allowances by distorting the raw edges. If you choose this method, skip Step c below.

a. Clip (page 142) about every ½" (1.3 cm) along any curves in the seam allowances, being careful not to cut into or through any seamlines (**fig. A**).

b. Press the seam open.

c. Set your sewing machine to a zigzag stitch, 1.5 mm long × 3 mm wide. Fold the main portion of the garment out of the way, leaving only one seam allowance under the machine's presser foot, and zigzag near the raw edge along the entire length of the seam. Turn the garment and repeat to zigzag along the remaining seam allowance edge. Press the seam open once again.

d. Adjust the needle position to a point ¼" (6 mm) from the presser foot's left edge and align the left edge with the seamline. Set the machine for a straight stitch 3 mm long. Sew along the entire seam, using the seam as a guide, tacking the seam allowance to the garment as you go (see **fig. B**). Continue stitching across any gaps created by clipping. This stitching will be visible on the outside of the garment, so keep it neat and straight!

e. Turn the garment around and repeat Step d to tack the remaining seam allowance to the garment (**fig. B**). From the right side of the garment, you will see two parallel lines of stitching bracketing the seam (**fig. C**). This finish will not only keep the seam allowances from raveling in the wash, but will provide a smoother finish inside the garment against sensitive skin.

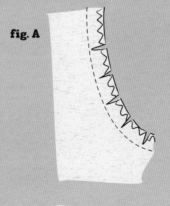
fig. A

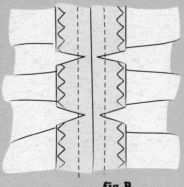
fig. B

fig. C

bread sharing
+ *homemaking*

Aren't we all homemakers? Regardless of your chosen profession, we all have a role to play in family life that makes our time together feel like "home." Homemaking implies a constant state of doing. Bread can be homemade, a decoration can be homemade, but a home is never in the finished state of being "made"! I highly value process over product when it comes to creativity, yet it seems more difficult to apply that ideal to homemaking. However, I've found that it's actually easier to maintain this state of mind now that I'm a mom.

You see, I don't do housekeeping. Housekeeping, to me, implies an unachievable state of keeping my home pristine, which I certainly can't do with a toddler, a baby, and a business to run. Homemaking? That I can do. I have little rituals such as baking bread on Tuesdays and making yogurt on Thursdays. I cut wildflowers for display on our dining table. I take care of the animals and maintain a small container garden. The best part is that my sons can do all of these things with me, and participating in the practical daily (or weekly) activities of caring for home and family helps young children develop physically, cognitively, and emotionally.

In this chapter, you will find a variety of projects that will help you to involve your children in the day-to-day tasks of homemaking, including an Embroidered Placemat (page 48), which helps children learn how to set the table, and a Silk Ring Sling (page 38), which allows you to keep very young children close as you go about your day.

silk ring
sling

Life with a young baby has its challenges, but wearing the baby in a sling while attending to daily necessities provides a balance for parent and child. Wearing my son Finn in a sling was one of the best decisions I made as a parent. It allowed me to go about my daily routine, while still keeping my son close and including him in my activities. Although it must be handwashed, the silk used in the sample is a great choice for this sling. It's cool in the summer, warm in the winter, and so lovely against a baby's skin.

FINISHED SIZE 26½" wide × 80" long (67.5 × 203 cm).

FABRIC + MATERIALS

- 2¼ yd (2.1 m) of 45" (114.5 cm) wide raw silk or other strong silk (see Notes)
- Two 3" (7.5 cm) sling rings
- Coordinating sewing thread

TOOLS

- Serger (optional)
- Walking foot for sewing machine (optional)
- Topstitch needle (size 90/14) for sewing machine (optional)
- Rotary cutter, quilter's ruler, and self-healing mat (optional for cutting)

notes

- Raw silk is soft but has a linen-like texture that grabs the rings securely. For this project, be sure to choose a similar silk (or alternate) fabric that is not slippery or overly delicate.

- I used organic Incandescent Peace Silk from NearSea Naturals for the sling shown. See Resources on page 158 for suggestions on where to find good silk (and sling rings).

- If the wrong side is indistinguishable from the right side, pick a side to be the wrong side and mark it in several places with masking tape or tailor's chalk.

- Remember to wash, dry, and press fabric before beginning.

Cut + Prepare the Fabric

1 Cut one 2¼ yd × 27½" (2.1 m × 70 cm) rectangle.

2 Press ¼" (6 mm) to the wrong side twice along all four fabric edges. Set the machine for a wide zigzag (3.0 mm long and 3.0 mm wide). Use a contrasting thread color so the hemming stitches become a design element. Pin the hem in place if desired, or work by simply tucking the raw edges under as you sew. Zigzag the hem, pivoting at the corners. If you have a serger, use the rolled-hem setting to finish all four edges of the fabric instead.

Form + Sew the Pleats

The pleats can be made in any configuration, as long as they control the fabric before allowing it to spread apart for cupping the shoulder. *The final width of the pleated fabric should be 3½" (9 cm).*

3 Fold one short edge of the fabric in half lengthwise to find the center. Mark the center with a fabric pen or tailor's chalk.

4 Measure 1½" (3.8 cm) to each side of the center and mark. Continue measuring and marking the solid lines shown in **fig. 01**. The two dashed lines closest to the hems represent the inner edges of the hems and need not be marked. Fold the fabric with wrong sides together at each solid line and press to crease for 2" (5 cm) below the hemmed short edge. Lay the fabric on a flat surface. Beginning with the creases closest to the center and working toward the sides, fold along a crease, wrong sides together, and bring the fold to meet the next crease (**fig. 02**). Pin in place. The last fold (solid line) on each side should be brought to meet the inner edge of the hem. Mark lines ½" (1.3 cm) and 1½" (3.8 cm) from and parallel to the short hemmed edge, marking across the pleats. Set the machine for a straight stitch and sew along each line to secure the folds.

Sew in the Rings

5 Slip the pleated fabric through both sling rings and fold 3½" (9 cm) of fabric to the wrong side around the rings. Working with the pleated end on top, pin the fabric layers together at the center, enfolding the sling rings. Spread out the fabric behind the rings so it extends 1½" (3.8 cm) beyond the pleated fabric on both sides and pin the short end to the spread fabric (see **fig. 03)**. Turn the sling over and ensure that the pleats on the right side of the sling are arranged neatly and free of unsightly bunching. Pin in place.

6 Use a walking foot, if available, for this step to make sewing through the bulky layers easier and more accurate. You may also use a special topstitch needle for this job to protect the thread as it passes through all the fabric layers. Sew across the entire shoulder width, using a straight stitch and contrasting thread, sewing as close to the rings as possible. The stitching line will curve, following the line of the rings, and should lie 1½–2" (3.8–5 cm) below the rings, approximately on top of the 1½" (3.8 cm) line of stitches from Step 4 (see **fig. 03**).

7 Sew a second line of straight stitches ½" (1.3 cm) below the first. Exchange the walking foot for a satin or decorative stitch foot or just use your standard (zigzag) foot; choose a decorative stitch (see your sewing machine manual and ensure that you choose a stitch that will work with the foot you have selected). Stitch across the shoulder again, placing the decorative stitch halfway between the lines of straight stitching. A decorative stitch has the double benefit of showing a lot of the contrasting thread and providing a very strong stitch, essential if you'll be carrying a precious baby who will depend on the strength of these stitches for his or her safety (**fig. 03**)!

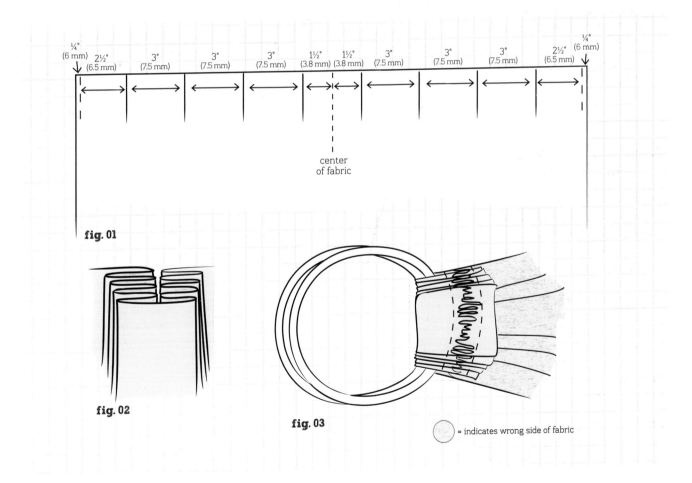

¼" (6 mm) 2½" (6.5 mm) 3" (7.5 mm) 3" (7.5 mm) 3" (7.5 mm) 1½" (3.8 mm) 1½" (3.8 mm) 3" (7.5 mm) 3" (7.5 mm) 3" (7.5 mm) 2½" (6.5 mm) ¼" (6 mm)

center of fabric

fig. 01

fig. 02

fig. 03

= indicates wrong side of fabric

the fabric slightly on your shoulder for comfort, but be aware that spreading the fabric too far can limit your movements.

9 Always put safety first. Before wearing your baby in the sling, be sure to check out the sidebar at right for instructions on how to use the sling to facilitate a few of the common "holds" for your baby. You can also look online for instructional videos.

8 Thread the tail (the unpleated short edge) of the sling through the rings as if you were threading a D-ring belt: through both rings from the back, then back through the lower ring only (**fig. 04**). Be sure the sling fabric is not twisted or knotted. Slip the sling over your head, keeping it untwisted, and position the rings on your chest just below one shoulder with the tail hanging down. As the fabric passes from the rings across the body to the opposite hip, a pouch or "bowl" forms. The baby will be cradled in the bowl. Spread

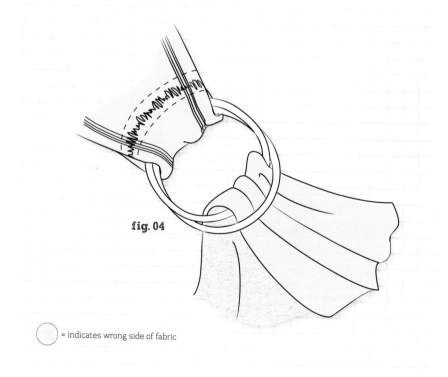

fig. 04

◯ = indicates wrong side of fabric

using your ring sling

There are multiple ways to carry your baby in a ring sling, with different options according to the age of the child and the preferences and comfort of both the child and the wearer/carrier.

Two "holds" are illustrated here to get you started, but you may also want to check the Internet for information on other "holds" and safety information. Some websites I would recommend for this purpose are: *thebabywearer.com; babywearinginternational.org;* and *mothering.com/green-living/babywearing-101.*

• Before carrying your baby/child in the ring sling, make sure you are wearing the sling properly. The sling should be worn over one shoulder, with the rings near one shoulder so that the sling wraps around the opposite side of your body (see **fig. A**), with the tail of the sling hanging down from the rings in front of you. The rings should lie in the "hollow" just beneath your collarbone, but every body is different, so adjust the placement until you find a comfortable placement for the rings near your shoulder (if the rings are too high, the weight of the baby will cause the rings to dig into your shoulder). Always exercise caution while wearing your baby. Make sure the baby is securely and comfortably cradled in the sling, but also ensure that the baby's breathing is not restricted in any way.

Cradle Hold

This hold is appropriate for a very young baby (newborn to 3 months). Refer to **fig. A**.

• Pull up the fabric of the sling that is closest to your body so that the sling is doubled in front of your body, creating a "pouch" of fabric to cradle the baby. Tighten the sling so that it lies snugly against your body.

• Place the baby in the pouch just created, with her head near the rings but facing away from them. She should be sitting upright (not lying flat), with her back supported by the sling fabric leading up to your shoulder. She should be sitting with her side resting against your body. You may

fig. A

need to cross her legs so she can sit in the sling comfortably. She should be cradled by fabric on both sides of her body.

• Support the baby's weight with your hand underneath her until you are sure that she is properly supported. Check to make sure that her chin is not pushed against her chest (this will restrict breathing; she should be slightly reclining) and that she is supported securely by the sling. Tighten or loosen the sling as necessary so that the baby is in the proper position. Ask someone to help you if this is difficult to do on your own.

fig. B

Hip Hold

This hold is appropriate for a slightly older child who can sit up without assistance (from about 6 months on). Refer to **fig. B**.

• Adjust the sling fabric opposite the rings so that it sits just above your hip (the hip opposite the rings). Pull up the fabric that is closest to your body so that the sling is doubled in front of your body, creating a "pouch." Spread the fabric at the rings and slightly loosen the outer portion of the "pouch" (farthest from your body).

• Bring the child's feet through the sling from top to bottom and allow his legs to cradle your hip (with one leg to the front and one leg to the back of your body). Seat the child in the "pouch" so that the sling fabric supports his back, bottom, and the upper portion of his legs. Adjust the fabric as necessary so that it forms a kind of "chair" so that the child can relax against the fabric at his back. The child's knees should be slightly above his bottom.

all-by-myself bib

When children are tiny, simple snap bibs can protect shirts from drool and spit-up. Older babies and toddlers need a bib to protect against spills and staining. But my son decided, at least for a while, that it was more fun to pull the snap bib *off* than to eat his food. My solution was this bib that slips over the head like a T-shirt with no weak fasteners to worry about. Because it has no behind-the-neck snaps, a slightly older child can pick it out and put it on all by himself! Plus, it's reversible—if one side gets dirty, simply turn it inside out and use the clean side.

FINISHED SIZE 12¾" long × 8½" wide (32.5 × 21.5 cm). Neck opening is stretchy. One size fits most.

FABRIC + MATERIALS

- ½ yd (46 cm) of 60" (152.5 cm) wide medium-weight cotton interlock knit
- ⅛ yd (11.5 cm) of 60" (152.5 cm) wide lightweight cotton rib knit
- Coordinating sewing thread

TOOLS

- All-By-Myself Bib pattern in pattern envelope
- Swedish tracing paper or other pattern paper
- Ballpoint or stretch sewing machine needle
- Fine ballpoint pins
- Rotary cutter, quilter's ruler, and self-healing mat (optional for cutting)

notes ✳

● ⅜" (1 cm) seam allowances are used unless otherwise noted.

● Remember to wash, dry, and press all fabric before beginning. Take care not to stretch the knit fabrics when pressing and cutting out the pieces.

● See Working with Knits on page 139 for information about the best stitches for seams in knit fabrics.

● Be sure to use the ballpoint or stretch needle on your machine for the entire project, as you will be sewing on knit fabric.

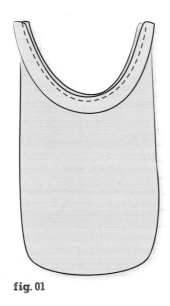

fig. 01

bib back

bib front

fig. 02

Cut the Fabric

1 Trace the pattern pieces onto Swedish tracing paper or other pattern paper, transferring all pattern markings, and cut out.

2 Fold the interlock knit fabric with right sides together, bringing the selvedges to meet at the center of the fabric. Cut two Bibs on the fold and transfer the notches to the fabric.

3 From the rib knit, cut two binding strips 1½" (3.8 cm) wide across the fabric width and remove the selvedges.

Sew on the Neck Binding

4 Sew the binding strips, right sides together, along one short edge. Press the seam open. From this seamed strip, cut two strips 11¾" (30 cm) long for the neck bindings and set aside the rest.

5 Using a narrow zigzag stitch and referring to the instructions under Attaching Ribbing to an Edge on

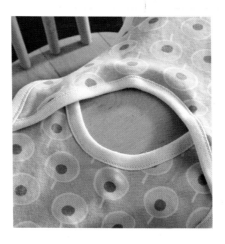

page 141, attach one Neck Binding to the neck edge of one Bib, right sides together **(fig. 01)**.

6 Press the Binding and seam allowances away from the Bib, using the iron's steam setting to ease the ribbing

into shape. Fold the Binding raw edge over the seam allowance, to the Bib wrong side, and press. The Binding raw edge will extend just below the seam on the wrong side of the bib. Pin the Binding in place.

7 From the front of the Bib, topstitch the Binding with a zigzag stitch just above the previous seam. The Binding raw edge on the bib wrong side will be caught in this seam, enclosing the seam allowances. The rib knit won't ravel significantly, and a raw-edge finish is much less bulky and more comfortable for a baby than a folded-under edge or an overcast or serged finish.

8 Repeat Steps 5–7 to attach the remaining Neck Binding to the second Bib.

Assemble the Bib + Finish with Binding

9 Match the upper edges of one Bib neckline to the notches on the shoulders of the second Bib so that one of the Bibs (we'll call this the Bib Back) overlaps the Bib Front. Angle the Neck Bindings as necessary so that the entire Binding raw end will be caught in the seam and pin the overlapped areas in place. Sew zigzag basting seams a scant ⅛" (3 mm) from the raw edge of the shoulders, securing the overlapping shoulders **(fig. 02)**.

10 Fold ½" (1.3 cm) to the wrong side on one short end of the remaining rib knit binding. Pin the binding to the bib, right sides together and raw edges matched, beginning with the pressed end at the straightest part of the Bib Back. Continue pinning the binding along the entire outer edge of the bib, leaving a short tail of binding to overlap the pressed end of the binding. Zigzag the binding to the bib, beginning at the pressed end and catching the fold in the seam. Continue stitching around the entire bib until you reach the fold once again, then stitch another ½" (1.3 cm) beyond the fold to secure the overlapped binding tail. Backtack (page 142) and cut off any excess binding.

11 Press the binding away from the bib and follow the instructions in Steps 6 and 7 to finish the bib.

mindfulness in homemaking with young children

Children learn by imitation and by doing, and involving children in homemaking makes them feel like important, contributing members of the family. So try focusing on the creative aspect of homemaking with children. Here are a few tips to get you started:

● Clean with children, don't clean while they're sleeping! It's best to spend that time relaxing, sewing, or reading a good book. Put up your feet! You'll be a better mama, daddy, grandparent, or caregiver if you've also taken some time for yourself. Plus, the shared activity is a great learning experience for the little ones.

● Use nontoxic, natural cleaners (safe for the whole family). It's amazing what white vinegar can do!

● Set up an area with the child's own supplies. This can be a low shelf with pegs or simple hooks where you can hang a work apron, a child-size broom and mop, and a cloth for dusting or cleaning. For activities that require more specific supplies, arrange a tray on a low shelf containing the necessary items for that task.

● Use the Ten-Minute Tidy technique: set your timer for 10 minutes (or less, with younger children) and give everyone a basket in which they can gather toys and other out-of-place items and return them to their places. In our house, we put on Woody Guthrie's "Pick It Up" song (on repeat; see Resources on page 158) and sing along as we work!

● Don't rush through a task, young children will be observing and absorbing your movements and attitude. When homemaking with children, budget in more time to complete a task and be okay with imperfection in the final result. You have to love those little fingerprints left on the window that a four year-old just washed!

embroidered
placemat

If you visit a Montessori nursery, you may be surprised by the peaceful and precise way in which the toddlers help prepare the snack table. They lay out placemats (similar to the one shown here, though perhaps simpler) with the place settings outlined. Then they retrieve a flat-bottomed basket with two handles and bring over utensils in the basket, one type at a time. The magic of this purposeful activity is in the placemat itself—it provides a guide to help the toddler remember what has not yet been retrieved from the cabinet. With this embroidered version, a toddler can help set the table at home with her very own placemat!

FINISHED SIZE 18" × 13" (45.5 × 33 cm).

FABRIC + MATERIALS

Materials listed will make one placemat

- 1 fat quarter of cotton or cotton/linen blend fabric for placemat front (Main; *shown:* brown)

- 1 fat quarter of cotton flannel for placemat details (Contrast; *shown:* yellow print)

- ¼ yd (23 cm) of 45" (114.5 cm) wide cotton flannel for binding (*shown:* blue print)

- ⅝ yd (57.5 cm) of 15" (38 cm) wide Jiffy Grip fabric for nonslip backing (see Notes)

- Paper-backed fusible web for reverse appliqué

- 13" × 18" (33 × 45.5 cm) adhesive tear-away stabilizer (such as Sulky Sticky)

- Embroidery floss (*shown:* blue)

- Sewing threads to coordinate with Main and binding fabrics

TOOLS

- Embroidered Placemat templates in pattern envelope

- Handsewing needle with large eye

- Rotary cutter, quilter's ruler, and self-healing mat (optional for cutting)

notes

- ½" (1.3 cm) seam allowances are used unless otherwise noted.

- If you are unable to find a fat quarter of your chosen fabric, purchase ½ yd (46 cm) instead.

- Jiffy Grip fabric is sometimes sold as precut 11" × 24" (28 × 61 cm) pieces. If you cannot find a larger piece, purchase two precut pieces and sew them together to make a 21" × 24" (53.5 × 61 cm) rectangle, which you will later cut to size.

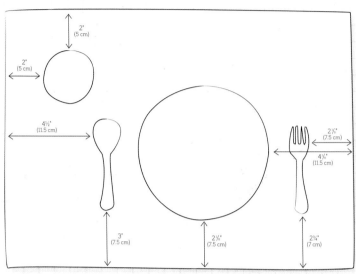

fig. 01

Cut the Fabric

1 Cut one 18" × 13" (45.5 × 33 cm) rectangle from each of the following: Main fabric, paper-backed fusible web, Contrast fabric, and Jiffy Grip (or other backing fabric).

2 From the binding fabric, cut two strips, each 2½" (6.5 cm) × width of fabric. Sew the two strips, right sides together, with a diagonal seam (page 144). Press the seam open, then use the joined strips to create double-fold binding following the instructions on page 144. Set the binding aside for now.

Reverse Appliqué + Embroider the Placemat Front

3 Trace the template pieces onto the paper side of the fusible web, using **fig. 01** as a guide for placement of each element. The pattern templates for the fork and spoon are already reversed.

4 Following the manufacturer's instructions, use your iron to adhere the fusible web to the wrong side of the Main fabric rectangle. Be sure the webbing is completely adhered to the entire fabric rectangle; if necessary, increase the heat of the iron and press again. With the paper still intact, use a pair of sharp embroidery scissors to cut out each design element, cutting through both the paper and fabric. Cut out carefully, especially around the prongs of the fork, and cut only the areas inside each element's outline. Remove the cut-outs and discard. Carefully peel away the paper backing, revealing the fusible adhesive.

5 Place the prepared Main fabric rectangle on the Contrast fabric, with both pieces right side up. Smooth the Main fabric and check that the fork prongs are properly arranged. Following the manufacturer's instructions, fuse the entire Main fabric rectangle to the Contrast fabric.

6 Remove the paper backing from the tear-away stabilizer and adhere it to the wrong side of the Contrast fabric. Thread the machine with thread that matches the Main fabric. For a sturdy finish to the appliqué, set the machine for a zigzag stitch 1.5 mm wide and 0.2-0.4 mm long. Test the stitch on scrap fabric and choose a length setting that provides full coverage without bunching the stitches. Turn the placemat front right side up and begin stitching along the edges of each shape. Position the needle and presser foot so that the needle's left swing enters the fabric just inside the shape through the Contrast fabric only. The right swing will enter the Main fabric, enclosing the raw edges in the satin stitch. Sew along all of the raw edges (fork, plate, spoon, and cup cut-outs). When the satin stitch reverse appliqué is finished, tear away the stabilizer, being sure to tear away the tricky spots inside the design elements, too.

7 Thread a handsewing needle with six strands of embroidery floss.

:: tip
Try allowing your child to use real glasses and breakable ceramic dishes when setting the table. While it's likely that something will fall and break one day, it's also a lesson in moving carefully and with grace. Next time, the child will be even more careful with her movements. If you'd like a slightly sturdier option, give the child a thick votive candleholder or a heavy-bottomed shot glass to use as a drinking glass for this activity. Another option is to purchase a child-size place setting specifically for your child; Michael Olaf (see Resources on page 158) carries beautiful child-size place settings.

Embroider a large running stitch (page 143) around the fork, plate, spoon, and cup, positioning the embroidery ¼" (6 mm) outside each design element. Sew straight across the top of the fork, ignoring the tines.

Assemble + Finish the Placemat

8 Lay the placemat backing (Jiffy Grip fabric) on a flat surface, textured side down, then smooth the assembled placemat front, right side up, on top of the backing. Pin the layers together to prevent shifting. If necessary, follow the instructions under Squaring Up on page 145 to trim the placemat edges into a uniform rectangle.

9 Follow the instructions for Attaching Binding with Mitered Corners on page 144 to bind the placemat edges with the double-fold binding made in Step 2.

learning through everyday tasks

In the Kitchen

As a mother and a former early childhood Montessori educator, I have found that young children are "sponges," eagerly absorbing everything from language to manners, without any conscious effort. I say, if the child is a sponge, then he or she belongs in the kitchen!

So many benefits are afforded the child who consistently spends time alongside mama or daddy as a meal is prepared. Children can begin helping in the kitchen as toddlers and continue to participate according to ability as they grow older. **Your young sous-chefs will gain many benefits from their kitchen experiences, including:**

- An appreciation of the origins of meals and the labor of love required to prepare them
- A willingness to try new foods that he or she has helped to prepare
- The feeling that he or she is an important, contributing member of the family
- Experience with fun sensory activities such as pouring, stirring, and kneading
- Practical math and science skills
- Logical thinking skills

Reading Practice

There are many wonderful books about involving children in cooking and baking. My favorites are *Baking Bread with Children* by Warren Lee Cohen and, for older kids, Mollie Katzen's step-by-step illustrated cookbooks for children. See Resources on page 158 for more information.

Preparing the Kitchen for Little Chefs

With a bit of planning and tweaking, your kitchen can be a functional, cheerful, and child-friendly space. Here are a few ideas:

- For babies and toddlers, have a low cupboard where they have access to play-friendly kitchen items, such as ladles, wooden spoons, pots, and bowls. As your children grow, it's still great (if you have the space) to designate a cabinet just for the kids, containing their tableware, placemats, napkins, child-sized cookware, and eventually their own cookbooks.

- Make snacks more accessible by reserving the lower shelf in the refrigerator door for a small pitcher of water, milk, or juice and a portion-sized container of a healthy snack. Even toddlers can learn how to get their cup out of their cabinet, place it on a small table, retrieve the pitcher from the fridge, and poor themselves a glass.

- Keep the kitchen playful! We have a small kitchen, but instead of putting an adult-size table and chairs in the tiny kitchen nook, we opted to make it a kitchen play/art area. Ours is outfitted with a small table and chair, a shelf where we keep a water dispenser and activity trays for our son Finn and a beautiful wooden play kitchen, which we use to store his real kitchen items, as well as some fun things to enhance his imaginative play.

- For young children (about ages one to seven), the wisest kitchen investment you can make is purchasing a safe step stool (such as the Learning Tower, see Resources) that you can adjust according to the height of the child, which allows him or her to reach the counter and work by your side. It's great fun for kids to wash dishes, help you mix ingredients or knead bread, or simply observe what you're doing.

- Have a plan—the week goes much more smoothly (and we tend to eat more balanced meals) if I take the time to work out a meal and snack plan in advance. The best time for me to do this is on Wednesday afternoon, after we've picked up our vegetable, milk, and egg Community Supported Agriculture (CSA) shares for the week (find a CSA program in your neck of the woods at LocalHarvest.org). In the winter, when we aren't getting fresh fruits and vegetables, I have a more fixed meal plan that doesn't vary as much from week to week.

- Visit your food source. Children love learning about where their food comes from, so visit a local farm, dairy, and bakery. If you can, grow some of your own food, even if it's just greens. Even the pickiest eaters will warm up to food that they've grown and prepared themselves.

Baby Greens Garden

Kitchen work can begin in the garden! This simple project requires only a small amount of space, and even those of you with the brownest of thumbs can succeed!

- Obtain a small raised flower bed or various containers in which you and your child can sprinkle generous amounts of salad green seeds, such as a mesclun lettuce blend. Use a high-quality compost as your base, then sprinkle the seed on the soil. Hand-sprinkle a bit of soil on top of the seeds (just enough to keep the seeds from blowing away) and keep it well watered using a watering can until the seeds begin to germinate. Once the greens are about 4 inches (10 cm) tall, send out your kitchen helper with a gathering basket and scissors to cut off enough greens for a family salad, leaving 1 inch (2.5 cm) of plant to regrow. Rotate the area you harvest and reseed as necessary to have a fresh three-season supply of salad. Encourage an older child to take the reins of the baby greens garden by choosing the seeds in the spring and taking charge of everything, from planting and watering to daily harvesting.

CHAPTER THREE

inside *play*

Creative play is an incredibly important part of a child's development. In dramatic play, children not only have a good time, they also have a chance to explore social roles and interactions. When children follow their own rules of imaginative play and encourage one another to follow the rules, they develop important habits of self-control all on their own.

Creative play will happen naturally when you take a few easy steps to make your home a playful refuge. You can get started simply by clearing up all those toys that may have taken over your floor and resisting the temptation to turn on the TV. Once you've prepared the scene (see the Fostering Creative Play sidebar on page 85), you and your children will be excited to add a few handmade toys and learning materials to the mix, which is why this chapter focuses on toys and activities that you can create for your child with your sewing machine! The Little Amigo Cloth Doll (page 56) and Reversible Hooded Play Cape (page 80) will accompany your child on many an imaginary adventure, and Irresistible Numbers (page 70) is a fun way to start learning numbers.

little amigo
cloth doll

A handmade doll is likely to become the most special toy a child owns, one that plays a significant role in his emotional development. A simple cloth doll helps a child act out and process all of the experiences in his own life and the lives of those around him. When playing with a doll, a child practices different roles, from caretaker to friend and confidant. This soft cloth doll can be personalized with the desired skin tone, hair, and expression. You'll be rewarded for the time spent creating this doll by the delight of the recipient.

FINISHED SIZE 16" tall × 6" wide at hips (40.5 × 15 cm).

FABRIC + MATERIALS

For fabric requirements for doll's overalls and doll's shirt, see page 66.

- ½ yd (46 cm) of 60" (152.5 cm) wide cotton knit fabric in a flesh tone
- 1 yd (91.5 cm) of 2" (5 cm) wide thick cotton gauze tubing
- 3–4 oz (85–113.5 g) of the wool yarn of your choice for doll wig
- Mercerized cotton crochet thread
- About 24 oz of wool stuffing
- Sewing thread in white and a color to match the doll's skin tone
- Embroidery floss in colors of choice for eyes and mouth
- Beeswax crayons in warm flesh tones for rosy cheeks
- Brown colored pencil (optional for freckles)

TOOLS

- Little Amigo Cloth Doll pattern in pattern envelope
- 5" (12.5 cm) long doll-making needle
- Ballpoint or stretch needle for sewing machine
- Handsewing needle and thimble
- Tweezers
- Water-soluble fabric pen
- Very fine-point permanent waterproof pen (*recommended:* Pigma Micron pen)
- Glass head pins for visualizing eye and mouth placement
- Needlefelting needle for making the inner head core (optional)

notes

- ¼" (6 mm) seam allowances are used unless otherwise noted.

- It's always best to sew every seam twice when you're making a doll. Dolls shouldn't be delicate—they must be durable for play!

Form the Head + Shoulders

1 Cut a 30" (76 cm) length of tubing. If the tubing has right and wrong sides, begin with the wrong side out. Lengthen the machine's stitch to 4.0 mm and baste a row of stitching across the exact center, from one long edge to the other, across the width of the tubing. Pull the bobbin threads to gather the tubing, then tie the threads off tightly at each end (**fig. 01**).

2 Pull one end of the tube over the other end, turning the fabric right side out, so that the gathering stitches form a closed flower/starburst shape and the raw edges align. This creates a double-layered tube measuring 15" (38 cm) long, with one end closed (**fig. 02**). Set this aside for now.

3 Begin to form a ball from a small amount of the wool stuffing by rolling it between your hands. Optionally, use a needlefelting needle to make the ball firmer and more cohesive, but note that this technique works only with wool stuffing. Pierce the ball repeatedly with the needle using an up-and-down motion and turning the ball as you work. Keep fingers away from the very sharp barbed needles. You may find it helpful to use a foam pad under the ball as you begin to form it—this will help you protect your fingers and work surface by allowing the needle to pierce

fig. 01

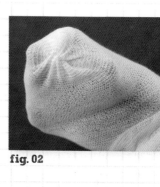

fig. 02

fig. 03

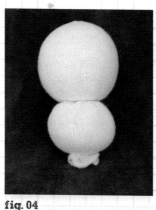

fig. 04

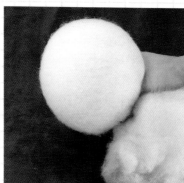

fig. 05

fig. 06

the foam pad under the ball. Once you have a ball that is large enough to pierce without endangering your fingers, continue felting without the foam pad (if you find it more comfortable to work over the foam pad, just be careful not to adhere the ball to the pad as you felt it).

Continue needling until the ball begins to felt and becomes more solid.

4 Wind strips of wool stuffing around the ball as tightly as possible. Continuing to use the needlefelting needle to secure newly wound wool to the ball is very helpful in keeping the ball firm; keep piercing the ball with the needle through the newly added wool. Continue adding wool until the sphere measures about 12" (30.5 cm) in circumference.

5 Arrange a handful of stuffing into a 17" (43 cm) square and place the wool ball in the center. Pull up the edges of the square and gather the wool into one hand, holding the wool tightly, to form the neck (**fig. 03**).

6 Continue to hold the extra wool tightly at the bottom of the ball as you insert the wool ball into the doubled tubing from Step 2. Center the gathers directly on top of the head. Use a 12" (30.5 cm) length of cotton crochet thread to tie off the bottom of the tube tightly just below the wool ball, keeping all of the stuffing inside. Smooth the tubing around the ball and tie another 12" (30.5 cm) length of crochet thread very tightly beneath the wool ball, enlisting an extra set of hands if needed, but don't make the neck too narrow. The result is a fabric-covered ball for the head, a tied-off neck, and a tied-off bulge beneath the neck, which will be used to form the doll's shoulders (**fig. 04**).

7 Fold the raw edges beneath the "shoulder" bulge inward, pushing the ends up toward the head with a finger. Pinch the folds together, flattening the shoulders from front to back and trapping the raw edges inside (**fig. 05**). Handsew the folded edges closed, using a whipstitch. It is easiest to begin in the center of these pinched-together edges and work toward one side, repeating from the center to close the other side. You will end up with a set of shoulders that looks somewhat like a scallop (**fig. 06**). The bottom edge will be curved, with the greatest distance between the neck and the bottom at the center of the shoulder piece.

:: finding materials for the doll + wig

To find the materials you need for doll making, check out the Resources on page 158. I recommend assembling your own materials rather than purchasing a doll-making kit—some of the kits available for making 16" (40.5 cm) dolls do not contain enough cotton knit fabric to make the doll from my pattern, as my doll is designed to look lovably chubby. However, there are kits available if you'd prefer to go that route; just be sure to check what the kit includes against the materials list on page 57.

Please experiment with your doll hair! Some people prefer the natural look of mohair or bouclé yarns and others prefer the more durable and whimsical look of a worsted-weight wool. Using a mixture of different kinds and colors of yarn is also an option that creates an interesting visual effect. For a very fun doll wig, take the future doll's little mommy or daddy to your local yarn store and let him or her pick out the color (or colors). A word of caution about bouclé, or "curly" yarn for hair: it sheds quite easily! This type of yarn should be reserved for use on a doll made for an older child who won't be tugging at it.

Add Facial Outlines to the Head

8 Form the eye line by wrapping cotton crochet thread or other heavyweight thread around the head as follows. Decide which side will be the front of the doll's head and place it face down on the work surface. Tie a piece of thread around the circumference of the head, centered exactly from top to bottom. Wrap it around the head twice, pulling to indent the covered ball, and knot it firmly at the back of the head with a square knot (page 143). This indentation forms the eye line (**fig. 07**).

9 To form the chin line, use another piece of strong thread to divide the head vertically. Place the center of a length of thread at the top of the head, bring the tails down to cross underneath the chin (just in front of the neck and shoulders), then bring them back up to the top of the head, pull moderately tight, and tie a square knot on the top of the head. The eye line and chin line should lie perpendicular to each other on either side of the head (**fig. 08**). These intersections are the "ears."

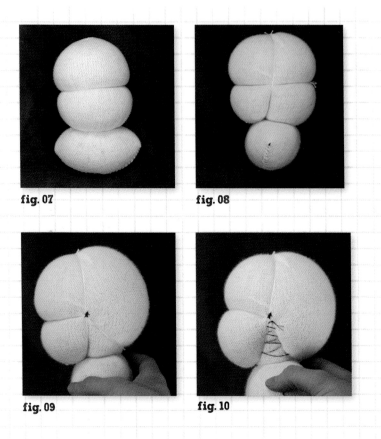

fig. 07 **fig. 08**

fig. 09 **fig. 10**

10 Thread the handsewing needle with white thread (shown in brown for clarity). At the junction of the eye and chin lines on one side of the face, whipstitch the two strong threads at each ear location, taking the stitches into the knit covering and catching a bit of the stuffing ball for security. Knot off. Repeat on the other side of the head.

11 Pull the back half of the eye line downward toward the neck, using tweezers or a crochet hook if necessary to grab the heavy thread. Reposition the back portion of the eye line ¼" (6 mm) above the neck string. Readjust the gauze along the neck if necessary and check to be sure there

is no unsightly bulging (**fig. 09**). Each head I make ends up having a slightly different shape, each eye line a slightly different arc. It's part of what gives each doll its distinct personality! I like to scoot the eye line in the front up ever so slightly, giving the doll more cheeks and an optimistic gaze.

12 To keep the thread from shifting, take a few long stitches between the eye and chin lines, just below the ears on either side of the head (**fig. 10**).

13 To make a nose, draw a ⅝" (1.5 cm) diameter circle just underneath the eye line in the center of the face with a water-soluble fabric pen.

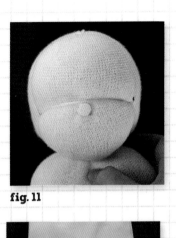

fig. 11

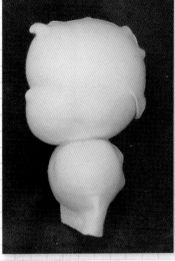

fig. 12

fig. 13

14 Picture the nose circle as a clock face for the following instructions, visualizing the top of the circle as 12 o'clock, etc. Thread the handsewing needle with white thread and knot the end of a length of doubled thread. Bury the knot in the head by inserting the needle near one ear and bringing it to the right side at the nose circle; a sharp tug on the thread will pull the knot to the head's interior. To prevent the knot from slipping through the gauze, sew a short straight stitch (page 142) at 12 o'clock. Reinsert the needle at 12 o'clock and bring it to the right side at 6 o'clock. Tug on the thread a bit to tighten; the object is to gather the nose into a small button nose shape with the stitches. Insert the needle at

7 o'clock and bring it out at 1 o'clock. Insert the needle at 2 o'clock and bring it up at 8 o'clock. Continue around the circle in the same fashion, giving each stitch a gathering tug, until you bring your needle up once again at 12 o'clock. Make sure the nose is well gathered and knot off the thread, burying the knot in the head. You should have a cute little button nose (**fig. 11**).

Sew the Head/ Shoulder "Skin"

15 Fold the cotton knit fabric lengthwise, with right sides together, creating a double thickness 2" (5 cm) wider than the head core. Lay the doll head on its side on the fabric, with the nose touching the folded edge

and one ear against the fabric. With a fabric pen, draw a stitching line around the head as shown in **fig. 12**, leaving a ½" (1.3 cm) space between the line and the head. Draw the neck indentation slightly lower than the actual neck, as this curve will ride up once the fabric is placed over the inner head. Continue the stitching line downward to the fabric edge; there will be no stitching line under the shoulder area.

16 Roughly cut a rectangle of fabric around the head outline, leaving 1" (2.5 cm) or more of space around the stitching line.

17 With the ballpoint needle in your sewing machine, set the machine to a zigzag stitch, 1.4 mm wide and 1.3 mm long. Sew directly on the stitching line through both thicknesses of the fabric, leaving the bottom edge open. Sew once again just outside the first line, reinforcing the seam. Cut around the sewn head/shoulders, leaving a ¼" (6 mm) seam allowance. Turn the head/shoulders right side out and slide it over the head/shoulder core. The seam should lie along the center of the head, from the top of the forehead to the back of the shoulders. Pull the fabric taut so that it clings to the eye line indentation. Smooth out the fabric around the neck. Tie another piece of strong thread around the neck, knotting it at the center back (see **fig. 13** for an example of the doll at this stage). Cut a very thin strand of cotton knit "skin" fabric, ½" (1.3 cm) wide across the stretchy crosswise grain and 5½" (14 cm) along the less stretchy lengthwise grain. Fold the strip in half lengthwise so that it is ¼" (6 mm) wide. Wrap it around the neck, covering the thread tied there, then overlap and sew the ends together at the back of the neck with a few whipstitches.

18 Smooth the fabric along the head seam, pulling the excess fabric into one or two points. Fold back the point (or points) of excess fabric and tack the excess fabric to the head with whipstitches (**fig. 14**); the work will be covered by the doll's hair, so pulling the fabric smooth and flat is more important than neatness.

19 Fold the open edges at the bottom of the "skin" inward and pinch the edges together. Sew the edges together to close the "skin," as in Step 7.

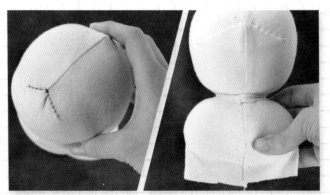

fig. 14

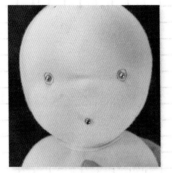

fig. 15

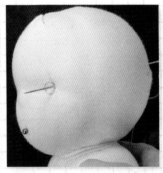

fig. 16

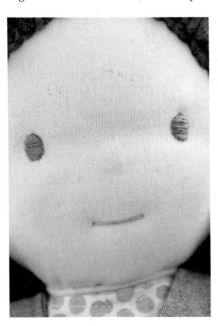

Embroider the Eyes + Mouth

20 Place three glass-head pins in the doll head to mark the eyes and mouth locations: two along the eye line and one centered below the nose. Now, fiddle around with the pins—are they in the right spot for this doll? Should the eyes be farther apart or closer together? A good rule of proportion is to envision an equilateral triangle formed by the two eyes and mouth. Once you're happy with the

placement, use a very thin permanent pen to carefully draw circles around the eye pins. You will be filling in the circles with embroidery thread (**fig. 15**). Remove the eye pins.

Picture each eye circle as a clock face for the following instructions, visualizing the top of the circle as 12 o'clock, etc.

21 Thread a long doll-making needle with two strands of the embroidery floss you have chosen for the eyes. Push the needle through the back of the head, opposite one of the eyes, and through the inner head core until the tip comes out exactly at 3 o'clock on the eye circle (**fig. 16**). Pull

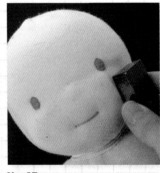

fig. 17

the floss through, leaving a 3" (7.6 cm) thread tail at the back of the head, and remove the doll needle. Thread the floss through a handsewing needle and proceed to embroider the eye with a satin stitch (page 143), beginning in the middle of the circle (3 o'clock to 9 o'clock) and moving outward with parallel stitches. Once you are done, replace the handsewing needle with the doll needle and pull the thread through to the back of the head, knotting off at the back of the head by tying the two tails together securely. Bury the thread tails in the head core. Repeat entire step to embroider the other eye.

22 To embroider the mouth, make one long horizontal straight stitch centered on the mouth pin, following the same method as above, except this time using four to six strands of embroidery floss.

23 Use a beeswax crayon to give the doll rosy cheeks by gently rubbing the crayon over the doll's cheeks in a circular motion. Add some freckles with a brown colored pencil if desired (**fig. 17**).

Make the Body

24 Fold the remaining cotton knit fabric in half, right sides together, and lay the Arm and Torso/Legs pattern pieces on the fabric, leaving at least 1" (2.5 cm) between pieces. Arrange the patterns with the grainlines along the fabric's lengthwise grain; the direction with the most stretch will run across the pattern pieces from side to side. Use a water-soluble fabric pen to trace around the pattern pieces, transferring all markings. The traced lines are the stitching lines, so accuracy is important. Do not cut out the pieces; instead, use pins around the traced lines to keep the fabric from shifting while you sew. Roughly cut the doubled fabric around the Arms and Torso/Legs, leaving at least ½" (1.3 cm) around each pattern piece.

25 Make sure that you have a ballpoint needle in the sewing machine and set the machine for a zigzag stitch 1.4 mm long and 1.3 mm wide. Sewing directly on the marked line and beginning at the underarm notch on the torso, stitch down the leg, up to the crotch, down the other leg, and up to the second underarm mark. Stitch again just outside the first stitches to reinforce the seam.

26 Sew the arms as in Step 24, starting at the neck opening notch and continuing around the entire arm unit until you reach the opposite neck opening notch. Reinforce the seam as before.

27 Cut out the torso and arm pieces, leaving a ¼" (6 mm) seam allowance. Use embroidery scissors to clip along any tight curves (such as the thumb and the crotch) but be very careful not to cut into the seam. Turn the arm unit and torso/legs right side out.

28 Begin stuffing the arm unit. Pull off small bits of wool at a time to keep lumps from forming. Stuff firmly, beginning with the thumb and fingers. Stop stuffing when the wool reaches the neck opening. Stuff the other arm in the same way, then insert the head/shoulders into the neck opening in the arm unit. Check to make sure there isn't any space without stuffing, then use a whipstitch to attach the arm unit to the shoulders. Stitch securely, without regard for neatness; these stitches will be covered by the torso (**fig. 18** on page 64).

29 Stuff the legs in the same way as the arms, stuffing firmly until you reach the junction of the legs/torso. Leave this area sparsely stuffed, as you want the legs to be able to move so the doll can sit. Once both legs are stuffed to this point, sew a straight seam across the top of both legs (**fig. 19**). Continue stuffing the torso. I like a firmly stuffed belly, but the belly shouldn't be quite as firm as the arms and legs. Stuff until you reach the underarms/top of the side seams.

30 Insert the shoulders/arms into the torso, adding a bit more stuffing around the shoulder/arms unit. Fold ¼" (6 mm) to the wrong side along the tops of the torso pieces and pin the folds just under the neck. Continue folding ¼" (6 mm) to the wrong side along the torso upper edges/shoulder seams and pin the front and back torsos together over the shoulder unit. Fold ¼" (6 mm) to the wrong side along the remaining torso edges and pin the folds to the arm unit front and back (**fig. 20**).

31 Using a small whipstitch and matching thread, sew the torso to the head/shoulders and arms. Begin handsewing at the outer corner of one shoulder and continue across the top of the shoulder, around the front neck, and across the top of the other shoulder. Pass the needle under the shoulder just sewn and continue sewing along the back neck. Knot and cut the thread, pulling the excess thread underneath the fabric.

32 Use a whipstitch to sew the torso fabric to the arm unit around each arm, starting at the shoulder seam.

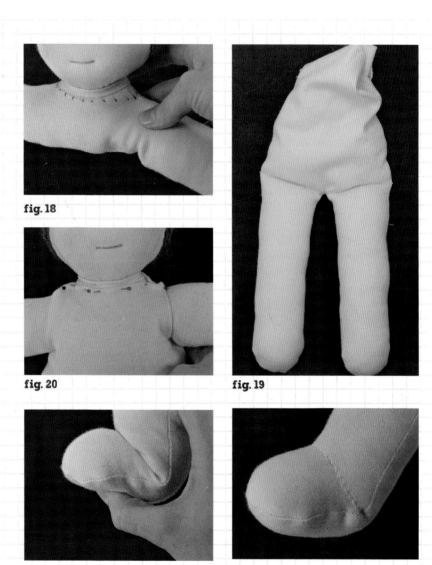

fig. 18

fig. 20

fig. 19

fig. 21

fig. 22

33 To shape a foot, push the toes upward and to the front, at a right angle to the leg, tucking the excess fabric into the crease to form a dart (**fig. 21**). Slip-stitch (page 143) across the crease, keeping the foot in this position, by alternately taking one stitch in the foot fabric and one in the leg. Knot the thread well to secure the

:: tip

For a tutorial on creating durable crocheted doll wigs, visit my blog at **sewliberated.typepad.com/dollhair.html**. Crocheted wigs are a great option for creating wigs for both boy and girl dolls.

stitching (**fig. 22**). Repeat to shape the second foot.

Make the Doll Hair

34 Using tailor's chalk or a fabric pen, mark a hairline around the doll's head, following the line of the forehead, "ears," and the nape of the neck (**fig. 23**).

35 Thread a needle with a strand of the wool you chose for the doll's hair. Starting from the marked hairline, use closely placed stitches, about ⅝" (1.5 cm) long, to cover the scalp (**fig. 24**). These rows of stitches will keep the scalp fabric from peeking through once the hair is applied. For a short-haired boy doll, you can pack these stitches very closely together to make a fuss-free wig, omitting Steps 36–37.

36 To make longer hair, experiment with the desired length by draping a strand of wool over the center of the doll's head, where the center part will be. Once you have chosen the length (perhaps 28" [71 cm]), cut three bunches of 45–50 wool strands each to this length; the exact number of strands per bunch will vary with the yarn's weight. Each bunch should fit easily on the crown of the head along the center part.

37 Center the first bunch of hair on the head so that an equal length of wool falls to each side of the head. Handsew this bunch to the head along the center part using small stitches and coordinating cotton thread (**fig. 25**).

38 Evenly distribute the hair around the back of the head so that the back and sides of the head are covered by this long hair. Using a backstitch (page 143), handsew the

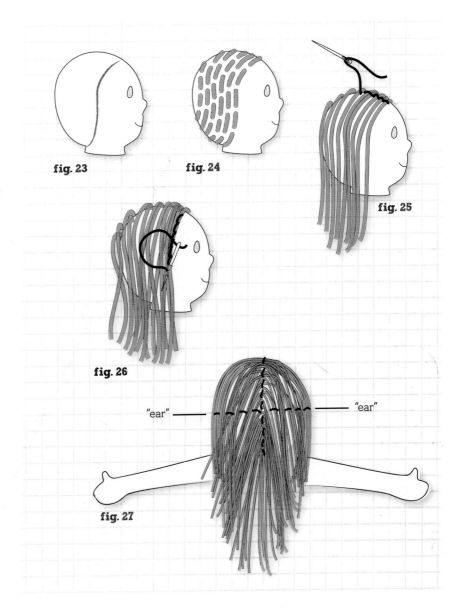

fig. 23

fig. 24

fig. 25

fig. 26

fig. 27

"ear" — — "ear"

strands to the hairline (where the embroidered stitches meet the face/neck; **fig. 26**).

39 Repeat steps 37 and 38 to attach the second bunch of hair to the center part. This time, handstitch the hair to an invisible line that goes around the back of the head, from "ear" to "ear" (**fig. 27**).

40 Repeat Step 37 to sew the final bunch of hair to the center part, leaving the rest of the strands free this time; this final bunch of hair will hide the stitching across the back of the head from Step 39. Trim the doll's hair to the desired length.

little amigo
doll clothing

FABRIC + SUPPLIES
little amigo overalls
- Little Amigo Overalls pattern in envelope

- ½ yd (46 cm) of 45" (114.5 cm) wide denim or other sturdy fabric, such as wool or corduroy

- 2 size 15 or 16 snaps and snap press (often available together as a kit)

- Hammer for attaching snaps

- Coordinating sewing thread (orange or yellow works well if you want to mimic jeans topstitching)

- Serger (optional)

little amigo shirt
- Little Amigo Shirt pattern in envelope

- ½ yd (46 cm) of 45" (114.5 cm) wide cotton print fabric

- Two small sew-on snaps

- Coordinating sewing thread

Make the Overalls
Assemble the Overalls

1 Trace the pattern onto Swedish tracing paper or other pattern paper, being sure to transfer all markings, and cut out.

2 Fold the fabric along the lengthwise grain, with right sides together, folding one selvedge toward the center just enough to create a doubled layer of fabric large enough for the Overall pattern piece. Cut one Overall piece on the fold, then repeat the folding with the second selvedge to cut a second Overall piece.

3 Zigzag stitch or serge along the outer edges of both Overall pieces.

4 Pin the Overall pieces right sides together and sew along both midline/crotch seams as shown (**fig. 01**). Clip the fabric along the curves and press the seams open.

5 Positioning the seams just sewn at the center front and back, match the seams and sew from one leg opening to the other along the inseam (**fig. 02**). Clip the curves and press the seam open.

6 Press ⅜" (1 cm) to the wrong side along both underarm edges. Topstitch (page 142) ¼" (6 mm) from the fold along the underarm curves to secure the hems. Repeat this process to hem the top straight edges of the front and back. Press ½" (1.3 cm) to the wrong side along each leg opening and topstitch as before.

7 From the remaining fabric, cut two rectangles measuring 6" × 2" (15 × 5 cm) for the overall straps.

8 Fold one overall strap in half lengthwise, wrong sides together, and press. Open the strap and fold each long edge to the wrong side so the raw edges meet at the center crease; press the new folds.

Press one short end ⅜" (1 cm) to the wrong side. Refold along the original center crease, enclosing the raw edges, and press again. Topstitch along all edges a scant ⅛" (3 mm) from the edge. Repeat entire step with the second strap.

9 Follow the manufacturer's instructions to attach the female components of the snaps ½" (1.3 cm) from the finished (folded) short end of each strap. Repeat to attach the male component of the snaps to the wrong side of the overall front, centering the snaps ½" (1.3 cm) from the top and side edges.

10 Put the overalls on the doll and snap the straps to the overall front. Pin the unfinished edges of the straps to the back top of the overalls so that the straps are on the wrong side of the garment. Adjust the strap placement for the best fit for your doll. Remove the overalls and sew the straps to the back of the overalls, stitching over the previous topstitching and again ⅛" (3 mm) below the topstitching, and backtacking at the beginning and end of each seam.

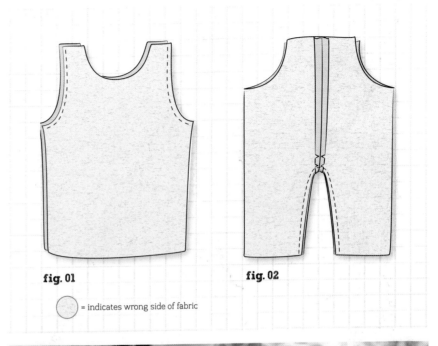

fig. 01 **fig. 02**

= indicates wrong side of fabric

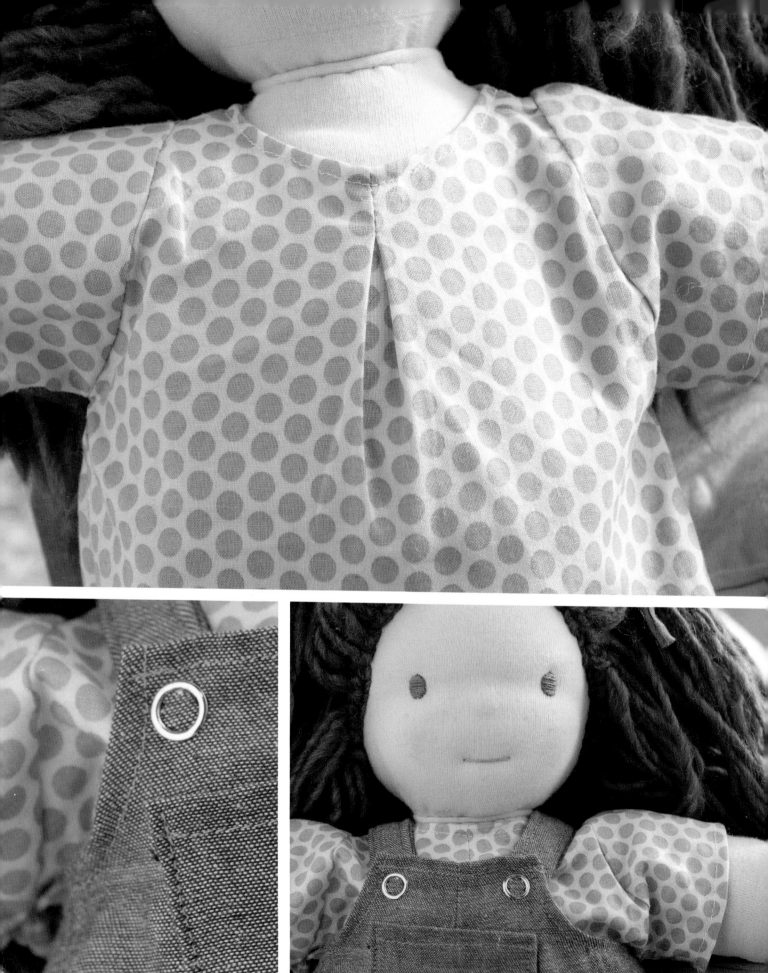

Add the Pocket

11 From the remaining fabric, cut a rectangle measuring 3" × 2¼" (7.5 × 5.5 cm). Press ¼" (6 mm) to the wrong side along the two short edges and one long edge. Fold ⅜" (1 cm) to the wrong side on the remaining long edge, press, and topstitch a scant ¼" (6 mm) from the fold. This will be the top of the pocket.

12 Pin the pocket to the front of the overalls, 1" (2.5 cm) below the top edge and centered on the overall front. Topstitch the pocket to the overalls along the pressed side and bottom edges, stitching ⅛" (3 mm) from the folds.

Make the Shirt

13 Trace the patterns (Shirt Front/Back and Sleeve) onto Swedish tracing paper or other pattern paper, being sure to transfer all markings, and cut out.

14 With right sides together, fold one selvedge toward the center along the lengthwise grain, creating an area just wide enough to accommodate the long edge of the Shirt Front/Back pattern. Cut one Shirt Front/Back on the fold as indicated on the pattern piece; this is the Front. Cut two Front/Back pieces not on the fold; these are the Backs. Cut two Sleeves.

15 Serge or zigzag stitch along the outer edges of each piece: Front, two Backs, and two Sleeves. This will keep the fabric from raveling.

16 Fold the Front in half, right sides together, along the center front. Sew a short seam ½" (1.3 cm) from the fold, beginning at the neck edge and continuing for 1" (2.54 cm). Bring

the seamline to meet the center front, forming an inverted pleat, and press.

17 With right sides together, pin the Backs to the Front at the shoulders and sew each shoulder seam. Press the seams open.

18 Press ⅜" (1 cm) to the wrong side along the straight edge of one sleeve. Topstitch the hem ¼" (6 mm) from the fold. Repeat to finish the other sleeve. Hem the center edges of each Back piece in the same manner. Pin the sleeves to the armholes, right sides together, matching the underarm and side edges, and stitch.

19 With the shirt right sides together, align the underarm seams and side seams and pin in place. Sew from the bottom edge of one sleeve to the bottom edge of the shirt in one continuous seam (**fig. 03**). Repeat to sew the remaining underarm/side seam. Press the seams open.

fig. 03

◯ = indicates wrong side of fabric

20 Press ¼" (6 mm) to the wrong side along the shirt neckline and topstitch ⅛" (3 mm) from the fold. Repeat to hem the bottom of the shirt.

21 Handsew the female component of each snap on the left shirt back, sewing the snap onto the right side of the fabric. Sew the first snap ½" (1.3 cm) below the left back corner of the neck; sew the second snap 1" (2.5 cm) below the first snap. Repeat to attach the male component of the snaps to the wrong side of the opposite neck corner, matching the placements.

:: **tip**

Choose fasteners for the doll clothing that your child can easily use. Velcro is a good option for younger children, while buttons or snaps would be appropriate for a slightly older child.

"Pure mathematics is the world's best game. It is more absorbing than chess, more of a gamble than poker, and lasts longer than Monopoly. It's free. It can be played any-where—Archimedes did it in a bathtub."

—Richard J. Trudeau, *Dots and Lines*

irresistible

numbers

Craft this set of numbers for a child who is enamored with counting! Inspired by the sand-paper numbers in Montessori classrooms, these cloth versions can inspire counting fun in the home. The stitching around the numbers makes tracing them with a finger so enticing, and the number set will provide hours of fun for learning numbers (see pages 74–75 for suggested games/activities). Besides, making this project is a cinch—the sewing is minimal and the embroidery can be accomplished at a leisurely pace by working one number a night before you go to bed.

FABRIC + MATERIALS

- ☐ ½ yd (46 cm) of 45" (114.5 cm) wide light-colored linen/cotton blend fabric (such as Robert Kaufman Essex) for number rectangles

- ☐ ½ yd (46 cm) of 45" (114.5 cm) wide matching wool felt (or a wool/poly blend) for padding

- ☐ 9 small scraps of woven cotton fabric (for numbers 1–9)

- ☐ Scraps of fusible web to adhere numbers to backgrounds

- ☐ Coordinating cotton embroidery flosses

- ☐ Branch at least 1 yd (91.5 cm) long (if you don't have access to a branch, a wooden dowel can be used)

- ☐ Nine spring-type wooden clothespins (*shown:* multicolored clothespins from novanatural.com)

- ☐ 1½ yd (1.4 m) of ¼–½" (6 mm–1.3 cm) wide twill tape for hanging the branch

- ☐ Basting glue (Quilter's Choice)

- ☐ Carpenter's glue

- ☐ Hot glue gun and glue stick or high-tack craft glue

- ☐ Seam sealant (*recommended:* Fray Check)

TOOLS

- ☐ Irresistible Numbers templates in pattern envelope

- ☐ Rotary cutter, quilter's ruler, and self-healing mat (optional for cutting)

- ☐ Embroidery needle

- ☐ Chisel or flat scraper (optional; see Tip)

Prepare the Rectangles + the Numbers

1 Cut eighteen 5" × 4" (12.5 × 10 cm) rectangles from the cotton/linen fabric. This is most easily and quickly accomplished by cutting several layers at once with a rotary cutter, self-healing mat, and quilter's ruler. Repeat to cut eighteen rectangles of wool felt the same size. Set aside all but nine rectangles of the cotton/linen fabric.

2 Trace each number onto the paper side of the fusible web; the templates have already been reversed. Roughly cut around each number. Following the manufacturer's instructions, fuse one number to the wrong side of each cotton fabric scrap. Cut on the traced line, remove the paper backing, and fuse each number to the center of one cotton/linen rectangle. Using three strands of coordinating embroidery floss, embroider a stem stitch (page 143) around the edges of the numbers, placing the stitches on the colored fabric, just a millimeter or two from the number's edge.

Sew the Number Rectangles

3 Apply a thin line of basting glue to the wrong side of a plain cotton/linen fabric rectangle, ½" (1.3 cm) from each edge. Place a rectangle of wool felt on top. Apply the glue in the same way to the wool felt, adding another wool felt rectangle on top. Finally, apply the glue to the second wool felt rectangle and place a number rectangle, right side up, on

top. Repeat entire step to assemble the remaining number rectangles. Allow the stacks to dry for about an hour before proceeding. The basting glue's bond is not permanent but will keep the layers from shifting as you stitch through them.

:: tip

The bark on a branch may flake off, weakening the bond between the clothespins and the branch. To prevent this and ensure that the bond lasts, consider using a chisel or flat scraper to remove the bark from the branch before constructing the finished piece. Alternatively, choose a branch that features smooth thin bark, rather than one with thick rough bark. If you have a freshly cut branch, allow the branch to dry out before using it. This will allow you to assess the state of the bark before you attach the clothespins.

:: tip

You can also make a beautiful set of letters using the same instructions. To make a letter version, find a font that you like (preferably one with curved edges) and enlarge it to the desired size. Print and reverse each letter of the alphabet and use these instead of the number templates.

4 Sew around each rectangle ⅝" (1.5 cm) from the raw edges. With sharp fabric shears or a rotary cutter, trim the excess fabric ⅛" (3 mm) from the stitches; the finished number rectangles should measure 3" × 4" (7.5 × 10 cm).

5 Finish the edges of the rectangles with seam sealant, following the manufacturer's instructions.

Assemble the Branch Hanger

6 Arrange the nine clothespins evenly along the length of the branch. For a 1 yd (91.5 cm) branch, the space between clothespins will be about 3½" (9 cm).

7 Affix the clothespins to the branch with carpenter's glue, placing the glue just above the metal spring. Each clothespin should hang straight down from the branch; pins tilted backward will hold the numbers too close to the wall.

8 With three strands of embroidery floss, wrap the back of each clothespin to the branch tightly, creating a figure eight with the floss. Tie off securely at the back of the branch. Allow the glue to dry completely.

9 Tie the ends of the twill tape to the branch at least 1" (2.5 cm) from each branch end, knotting the twill tape securely. Apply a small amount of hot glue or craft glue (craft glue will require longer drying time) under each knot to secure them to the branch.

10 Attach one number to each clothespin and suspend the twill tape hanger from a hook so that the numbers hang at child-height for easy access.

irresistible numbers activities

Here are some ideas for using the Irresistible Numbers as a fun, interactive learning tool.

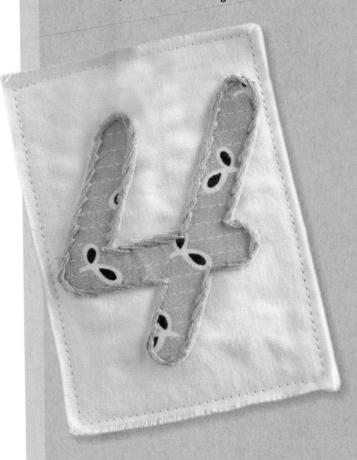

1 Naming the Numbers A young child who doesn't yet recognize the numbers can benefit from you casually naming the numbers. This will help the child gain a sense of counting before working intensely with the numbers.

a Three-Period Lesson Montessorians use this technique to help young children begin to learn the names of the numbers and associate the name with each number symbol. The "First Period" involves the child choosing a few numbers she wants to learn and bringing them to a flat working space. Then you will name them for her repeatedly. For example, you could say, "four," then trace the 4 with your finger. Then you might point to the 5 and say, "five." Identify each number in this way many times.

The "Second Period" is quite playful. You might say, "Hand me the four," "Put the five on my head," "Hide the three," "Trace the five," or "Put the four underneath the table." The possibilities are endless—if your child is active, take this opportunity to have her get up and move around, giving instructions such as, "Put the three next to the cat bowl" or "Hide the five underneath the pillow on the couch."

Spend some time doing just the first two periods of the lesson. Once you're fairly certain that your child will have success identifying the numbers by name, you can move on to the brief "Third Period." After a fun time moving the numbers around during the "Second Period," simply ask the child, "What is this?" and point to a number. If the child answers correctly, great! If not, then don't say anything—just return to working in the First and Second Periods. Eventually, everything will click!

b Knock-Knock Game + Variations Once your child recognizes most of the numbers, you can play the Knock-Knock Game. Have her bring the numbers she knows to a rug and place them face down. Show her how to "knock" on the back of the number and say, "Knock, knock, who's there?" Turn over the number, trace it with your finger, and say its name.

You can also work on the child's memory by asking her to bring you a certain number while you are sitting in a different room from the numbers. This presents a nice challenge for the young child, because she has to keep your request "in her head" as she goes to retrieve the number from another room.

2 Associating the Number Symbol with the Quantity Have the child bring a handful of numbers to a rug. Point to a number and say, "Bring me this many spoons" (or substitute any accessible objects, such as blocks, balls, books, etc.). This game is a source of endless fun and movement for the child. Another variation of this game is to hand the child a number he knows and ask him to "jump this many times," "give me this many hugs," "walk this many steps," and so on.

After having learned the sequence of numbers from lots of counting and games/activities, you can mix up the numbers and then ask the child to put to them in order on a rug. Have a small basket on hand containing forty-five small objects, such as paper clips, pennies, buttons, or the like. Show the child how to place one object underneath the 1, two objects underneath the 2, etc. Allow the child to take over. Periodically change the objects in the basket to renew the child's interest in this activity.

3 Tracing the Numbers These numbers are ideal for learning how to write numbers. Because the embroidery provides a perfect track for the little finger to follow, the child will develop a "muscular memory" of each number, which will eventually translate into writing the number on his own. Fun tracing games include:

- Tracing the number, then repeating the motions to "write" it on the table with a finger

- Tracing the number, then repeating the motions to "write" it in a sand-filled tray

- Tracing the number, then repeating the motions to "write" it on your back with a finger. You'll have to guess which number the child is tracing!

- Tracing the number, then repeating the motions to write it on a chalkboard

- Tracing the number, then repeating the motions to write it on a piece of paper with a pencil

4 Learning Teens, Tens + Larger Numbers Once your child learns the numbers 1–9, consider making another rectangle with the 0 symbol so that you can easily introduce the teens and tens in a similar fashion (as in suggestions 1–3) by just putting together two numbers.

As your child grows, she will still get a kick out of arranging the numbers in different ways on the clothespins and saying their names—for example, creating larger and larger numbers: "Four hundred and twenty-six million, nine hundred and eighty-one thousand, three hundred and fifty-seven!"

dress-up
bucket

Childhood just wouldn't be complete without playing dress-up! This Dress-Up Bucket is sturdy enough to hold plenty of accessories without flopping over, yet it is soft to the touch and perfect for use in play itself. Try rotating the items in the bucket every so often; children will be delighted when they find that a new (or forgotten) collection of dress-up items has appeared in the bucket. Attach a full-length mirror to a nearby wall, along with several pegs or hooks for hanging the Reversible Hooded Play Cape (page 80) and various thrifted garments for dress-up, and you've got the perfect (and super simple) setup for hours of imaginative play. You can even make up a few more buckets for storing stuffed animals or other lightweight items.

FINISHED SIZE 12" × 12" square × 10½" high (30.5 × 30.5 × 27 cm).

FABRIC + MATERIALS

✛ 1 yd (91.5 cm) each of two different 54" (137 cm) wide home decorator-weight cottons for shell and lining (choose two different but coordinating prints or colors for a look similar to the bucket shown; not suitable for directional fabrics)

✛ Coordinating sewing thread

✛ One 12" (30.5 cm) square and four 11¾" × 10" (30 × 25.5 cm) rectangles of ½" (1.3 cm) thick upholstery foam or densified foam (such as Nu-Foam or Tru-Foam)

TOOLS

✛ Swedish tracing paper or other pattern paper

✛ Dress-Up Bucket pattern in the pattern envelope

✛ Handsewing needle

✛ Zipper foot for sewing machine

✛ Rotary cutter, quilter's ruler, and self-healing mat (optional for cutting)

notes

- ½" (1.3 cm) seam allowances are used unless otherwise noted.
- Remember to wash, dry, and press fabrics before beginning.

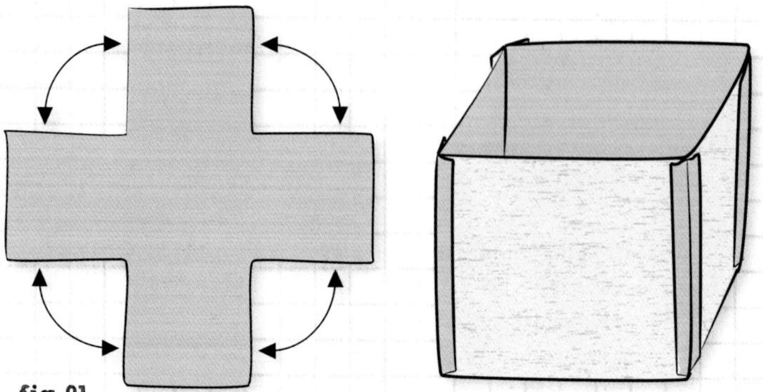

fig. 01

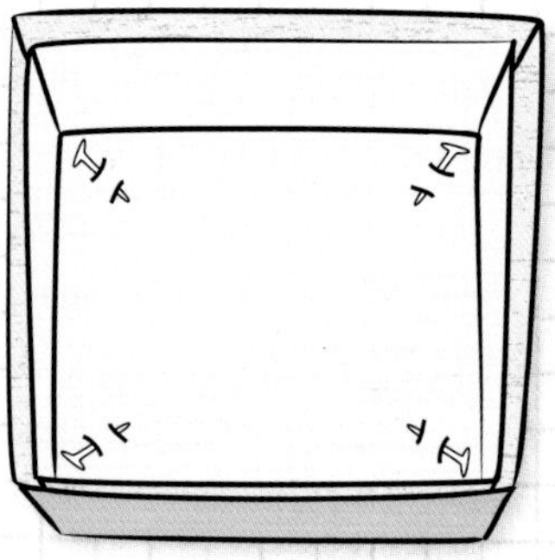

fig. 02

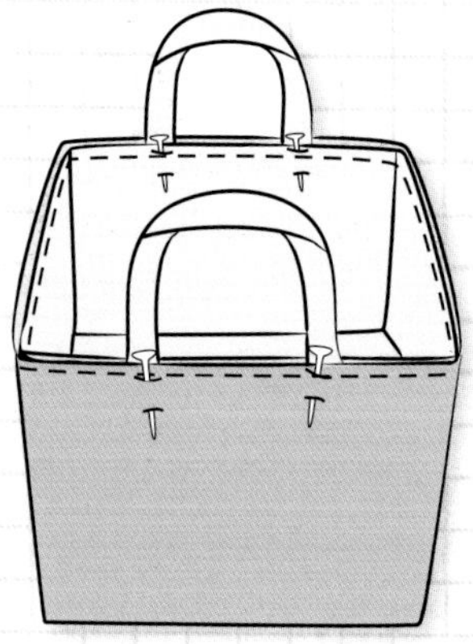

fig. 03

= indicates wrong side of fabric

Cut the Fabric

1 Trace the pattern piece onto Swedish tracing paper or other pattern paper, transferring all pattern markings, and cut out.

2 Fold the shell fabric in half lengthwise, with right sides together and selvedges aligned. Cut one Bucket on the fold, transferring the notches to the fabric. Repeat to cut one Bucket from the lining fabric. From the remaining lining fabric, cut two Straps, each measuring 11" × 3½" (28 × 9 cm).

Make the Straps

3 Fold one of the Straps in half, right sides together, matching the long raw edges. Pin and sew this edge, forming a tube.

4 Press the seam allowances open, arranging the seam so that it is in the center of the strap. Turn the strap right side out and press flat, making sure that the seam remains centered on the strap.

5 Topstitch (page 142) a scant ⅛" (3 mm) from both long edges.

6 Repeat Steps 3–5 to make the other strap, then set both straps aside.

Sew the Sides of the Bucket

7 Align two adjacent sides of the shell fabric Bucket, right sides together (see **fig. 01**), matching the notches, and pin. Sew this edge, starting at the raw top edges and continuing to the folded edge, which will become one bottom corner of the bucket. Repeat to form the remaining three sides of the bucket. Clip the corners (page 145) and press the seam allowances open. This completes the shell bucket, which is inside out (**fig. 01**). Repeat entire step to assemble the lining bucket.

8 Press 1" (2.5 cm) to the wrong side along the upper edges of the shell and lining.

Assemble the Bucket + Insert Bottom Batting

9 Turn the shell right side out. Insert the 12" × 12" (30.5 × 30.5 cm) square of foam into the bucket so that it is centered and resting on the bottom of the bucket. Place the lining inside the shell and align the side seams and the top raw edges, sandwiching the foam square between the two layers.

10 Smooth out the shell and lining fabrics along the bottom of the bucket, aligning the corners of

the shell and lining. Pin the foam in place from the inside of the bucket by pushing pins through all three layers: lining, foam, and shell (**fig. 02**). Turn the bucket over to view the bottom exterior and ensure there is no bunching in the fabric.

11 Thread a handsewing needle with coordinating thread and insert the needle between the Lining and Shell at one of the corners to bury the thread tail. Sew a large running stitch (page 143) all along the perimeter of the foam square, through the lining and shell, stitching as close to the foam as possible (without piercing the foam) to prevent shifting. Hide all knots between the lining and shell when you

need to start a new thread. The bottom foam should be held securely in place by the running stitches.

Insert Side Batting + Finish the Bucket

12 Insert one rectangle of foam into each side of the bucket, slipping it between the shell and lining with the long edges of the rectangle parallel to the bottom of the bucket. Position each rectangle as close to the running stitch seam as possible, and centered between the side seams.

13 Pin the shell and lining together along the entire top of the bucket, inserting the short ends of the straps along two opposite sides so that

each end of the strap is 3" (7.5 cm) from the nearest corner. Put an extra pin through the strap ends to hold them securely in place (**fig. 03**).

14 Attach the zipper foot to your machine and adjust the needle position as far to the left as possible (see your machine's manual—this may not be an option for your machine, and that's fine, too). Topstitch a scant ⅛" (3 mm) from the edge along the entire top of the bucket, catching shell, lining, and straps in the seam to finish the bucket.

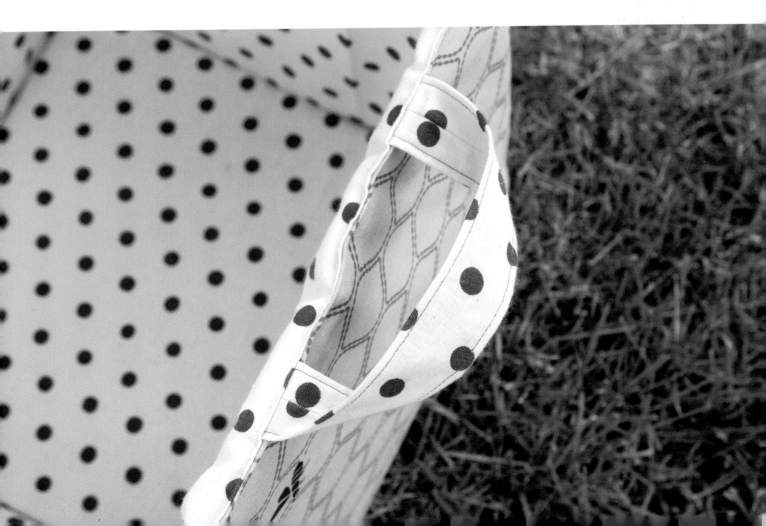

reversible hooded play cape

Donning this cape, a child transforms into Little Red Riding Hood, a member of the royal court, or a butterfly. Because it's reversible, it's even more versatile in a child's play. You may want to choose an animal-print lining (for your little animal lover) or make one side from a fuzzy, soft fleece—the sky's the limit! The elastic loop-and-button closure makes it easy to put on and take off. Hang it from a peg near the Dress-Up Bucket (page 76) for effortless storage and easy access.

FINISHED SIZE Size Small (Large) is 19½" (22¼)" (49.5 [56.5] cm) long from neck seam. Play cape is made to fit a range of sizes and will simply become shorter as the child grows taller. Size Small is made to fit ages 3–5, size Large is made to fit ages 6–8. Measure the child recipient to determine the best size.

FABRIC + MATERIALS

- ⅞ (1⅛) yd (80 [103] cm) of 60" (152.5 cm) wide woven cotton, silk, or silk/hemp blend fabric for shell (Main)

- ⅞ (1⅛) yd (80 [103] cm) of 60" (152.5 cm) wide woven cotton, silk, or silk/hemp blend for lining (Contrast)

- Coordinating sewing thread

- Swedish tracing paper or other pattern paper

- 3½" (9 cm) of thin elastic cord or "no metal" hair elastic

- 1⅛" (28 mm) button (*shown:* round wooden button)

TOOLS

- Play Cape pattern in pattern envelope

- Rotary cutter, quilter's ruler, and self-healing mat (optional for cutting)

notes

• ½" (1.3 cm) seam allowances are used unless otherwise noted.

• Remember to wash, dry, and press fabrics before beginning.

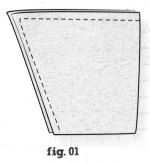

fig. 01

Cut the Fabric

1 Trace the pattern pieces onto Swedish tracing paper or other pattern paper, transferring all pattern markings, and cut out.

2 Fold the Main fabric in half lengthwise, with right sides together and selvedges aligned. Cut one Body on the fold and two Hoods, referring to the layout diagram on page 154 for assistance. Transfer all pattern markings, including the center point on the Body's neck edge. Repeat to cut the same pieces from the Contrast fabric.

Assemble the Cape

3 Place the two Main fabric Hood pieces right sides together and sew along the diagonal edge, then pivot with the needle down and continue sewing along the top (longer) edge (**fig. 01**). Clip the corner (page 145), turn the completed hood right side out, and press the seam open. Repeat to assemble the Contrast fabric hood.

4 Pin and then sew the Main fabric Hood to the Main fabric Body along the neck edge, right sides together, easing the hood to fit the neckline curve and matching the Hood's center back seam to the Body's center notch (**fig. 02**). Repeat to assemble the Contrast fabric Body and Hood.

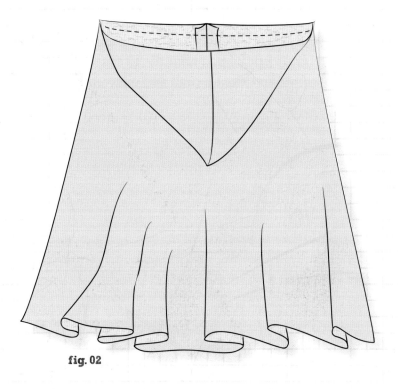

fig. 02

◯ = indicates wrong side of fabric

Finish the Cape

5 Form a loop with the elastic and place it on the right side of the Main fabric Body, ¾" (2 cm) below the neckline seam, positioning the elastic ends side by side and matching the raw edges. Baste the elastic in place ¼" (6 mm) from the raw edge.

6 With right sides together, align the neck seams, hood seams, and raw edges of the Main and Contrast capes and pin together securely. Sew along the entire perimeter of the cape, leaving a 5" (12.5 cm) gap for turning along the bottom edge of the cape body. Clip the corners (page 145) and clip the curved edges (page 145) to reduce bulk. Turn the cape right side out, pulling the elastic loop away from the body, and press, pressing the seam allowances at the gap to the wrong side. Topstitch (page 142) ⅜" (1 cm) from the entire edge of the cape body and hood, closing the gap.

7 Handsew the button to the edge of the cape just below the neck seam and directly opposite the elastic loop closure. Sew the button exactly on the edge so the cape can be easily reversed.

8 Take one or two small stitches through both layers of fabric at the very tip of the hood, hiding the knots between fabric layers. These stitches will keep the hood from bunching during movement and play.

:: **tip**

The rustic wooden button gives the Play Cape a woodlands mystique—I purchased mine from an Etsy seller (see Resources on page 158) but you could easily make your own if you have woodworking tools. Simply cut a slice from a branch and drill small holes through the center.

fostering creative play

Here are some ideas for creative play in your home:

● Reduce the number of toys on display. With too many toys available at any given time, children have a really hard time concentrating on their play. I've found it very helpful to have a small number of shelf toys available to my son, rotating them out for some of the toys in storage every few weeks. We've gotten more mileage out of each toy this way—when I pull a toy out of storage that he hasn't seen in a while, his interest in it is renewed, and he'll often come up with a new way to use it. *Simplicity Parenting*, by Kim John Payne (see Resources on page 158), outlines how to go about this monumental task of toy reduction.

● Set up play "stations" in every room you spend time in. Create a reading nook by placing children's books on a low shelf, with a comfy child-size chair nearby.

● Try setting up a space (and supplies) for your child to be creative near the space you use for your sewing and other craft projects. Your child will enjoy being near you as you both engage in favorite creative activities.

● Set up a doll-care play area and a dress-up basket in the living room or other living space that you use frequently. I've found that it's easiest, especially for young children, to locate their play in the living areas of the home, rather than in their bedroom. Children naturally prefer to play where their parents spend time.

● Incorporate simple, beautiful toys that are built to last. Toys such as blocks, pieces of fabric, and simple dolls encourage the child to use her own imagination to make the toys come alive. Simple toys tend to be more flexible for imaginative play than more structured toys, and they're easy to find or make yourself! Look outside to find free beautiful "toys" such as pinecones, acorns, seashells, and pretty rocks (for children who are no longer putting things in their mouths).

● Organize your play spaces using baskets and trays—it's easier for children to pick up at the end of the day if everything has an easily accessible "home."

CHAPTER FOUR

outside *play*

When adults hear the word "nature," it probably conjures up images of sweeping vistas, crashing waves, snow-capped mountains, and national forests. Nature is immense, perhaps far away, and for some of us, it takes quite an effort to get there—a car packed high with camping gear, a weekend reserved for a beach getaway, or a hike from a far-off trailhead. Of course, we know that spending time in nature is essential for children—it cultivates in them a sense of stewardship for the environment, helps sharpen their senses, and helps them learn about science firsthand.

Fortunately, children have a completely different experience of nature. For them, nature is small, intimate, and all around them. Young children especially cannot comprehend the immensity of a mountain, but they can come to love and appreciate the feeling of grass in between their toes and the wonder of ladybugs landing on their shoulders. A natural playground need not be a national park, it can be your own backyard. The important thing is that a child spend time in nature *daily*, in all kinds of weather (with proper clothing, of course). A backpacking trip once a year will certainly make for fond memories, but a true relationship with nature is cultivated by spending time in it, day in and day out.

Spending time outside every day is a wonderful way to add a bit of predictable *rhythm* to a child's life. Perhaps outside time can be right before lunch or following the after-school snack. In this chapter, you'll find some wonderful sewing projects that will help enhance outdoor playtime, from a portable art studio (Art Satchel, page 94) to a versatile and collapsible play tent (Hideaway Play Tent, page 108).

little amigo doll
papoose

Doll play shouldn't be restricted to the house, so this doll papoose is the perfect accessory! It allows your child to take her Little Amigo Cloth Doll (page 56) out for a walk in the woods, to Grandma's house, or to the doctor's office. My talented friend Fabiola Perez-Sitko designed this adorable papoose for her daughters and their dolls. Fabiola is a doll-maker extraordinaire, who sells her custom-made dolls and papooses at figandme.etsy.com, where her products fly out of her shop faster than she can make them. The Little Amigo Doll Papoose fits most 15- to 18-inch (38 to 45.5 cm) dolls.

FINISHED SIZE 13" wide × 20" long (33 × 51 cm).

FABRIC + MATERIALS

- ¾ yd (69 cm) of 45" (114.5 cm) wide heavyweight fabric such as corduroy or thick wool (Main; *shown:* dark brown corduroy)

- ¾ yd (69 cm) of 45" (114.5 cm) wide cotton fabric for lining and accent pocket (Contrast; *shown:* floral print on white)

- 16" (40.5 cm) of 1" (2.5 cm) wide cotton (or polyester) webbing for adjustable portion of straps (*shown:* black)

- 2 slide adjusters, 1" (2.5 cm) wide

- 1⅜ yd (126 cm) of 20" (51 cm) wide medium-weight fusible interfacing

- Swedish tracing paper or other pattern paper

- Seam sealant (*recommended:* Fray Check)

TOOLS

- Little Amigo Doll Papoose pattern in pattern envelope

- Rotary cutter, quilter's ruler, and self-healing mat (optional for cutting)

notes

- ¼" (6 mm) seam allowances are used unless otherwise noted.

- If using corduroy, cut the pieces with the nap (page 142) running in the same direction.

- The Papoose Back pattern piece includes dots for strap placement. Punch the holes through the dots on the paper pattern piece with a pen or an awl, then mark the fabric directly through the holes with a fabric pen or tailor's chalk; do not punch through the fabric. These will mark the placement for the strap ends.

Cut + Prepare the Fabric

1 Trace the pattern pieces onto Swedish tracing paper or other pattern paper, transferring all pattern markings, and cut out. Be sure to transfer all markings.

2 From the Main fabric, cut:
  ✳ One Back on the fold
  ✳ One Front on the fold
  ✳ One 25" × 5" (63.5 × 12.5 cm) rectangle, cut with the long dimension on the crosswise grain, for Visor
  ✳ Two 18" × 2½" (45.5 × 6.5 cm) rectangles, cut with the long dimension on the crosswise grain, for Straps

3 From the Contrast fabric, cut:
  ✳ One Back on fold
  ✳ One 25" × 5" (63.5 × 12.5 cm) rectangle for Visor
  ✳ Two 18" × 2½" (45.5 × 6.5 cm) rectangles for Straps
  ✳ One Front Pocket

4 From the fusible interfacing, cut:
  ✳ Two Backs on the fold
  ✳ Two 25" × 5" (63.5 × 12.5 cm) rectangles for Visor

Follow the manufacturer's instructions to adhere the fusible interfacing to the wrong sides of both Backs and Visors.

Make + Attach the Visor

5 Place the Contrast Visor and the Main Visor right sides together and sew one long edge. Turn the Visor right side out and press. Topstitch (page 142) ⅛" (3 mm) from the seamed edge. Topstitch again, ¼" (6 mm) from the seamed edge, for two parallel rows of stitching.

6 Press ⅜" (1 cm) to the Main fabric side along both short raw edges of the Visor and then set aside.

7 Press ⅜" (1 cm) to the wrong side along the straight upper edge of the Front. Fold and press another ¾" (2 cm) to the wrong side along the same edge.

8 Slip one pressed end of the visor under the pressed edge of the Front so the pressed allowances interlock, aligning the long raw edges (**fig. 01**), and pin. The Main fabric should lie right side up on both pieces. Repeat to connect the other end of the visor to the other side of the Front. With the unit wrong side up, topstitch ⅛" (3 mm) from the lower folded edge across the entire Front. Turn the unit right side up and topstitch ⅛" (3 mm) from the upper folded edge of the Front, catching the Visor in the stitching. There are now two parallel lines of stitching along the Front's straight edge (**fig. 02**).

9 Fold the Front in half, lengthwise, and pin-mark the center of the hemmed upper edge. Measure and mark the edge 1" (2.5 cm) to each side of the center point with pins. Fold the Front, wrong sides together, at each outer pin and bring the folds to meet at the center pin. Pin the inverted pleat in place, then secure it by topstitching over both of the previous stitching lines along the Front's upper edge (**fig. 03**).

Make + Attach the Pocket

10 Press ⅜" (1 cm) to the wrong side along the Pocket's straight upper edge. Fold an additional ¾" (2 cm) to the wrong side and press. Topstitch ⅛" (3 mm) from the inner folded edge of the pocket hem, then topstitch ⅛" (3 mm) from the upper fold, creating two parallel lines of topstitching (see **fig. 04**).

11 Staystitch (page 142) ¼" (6 mm) from the curved pocket edge. Clip the curved edge to the staystitching, but do not clip the stitches (**fig. 04**).

12 Press ⅜" (1 cm) to the wrong side along the curved pocket edge.

13 Pin the pocket to the Front, right sides up, centering the pocket 1½" (3.8 cm) above the bottom raw edge of the Front. Topstitch ⅛" (3 mm) from the entire curved edge, then topstitch again ⅜" (1 cm) from the same edge.

Make the Straps

14 Cut the webbing into four 4" (10 cm) lengths. *Press ½" (1.3 cm) to the wrong side on one short end of a Main fabric Strap. Center a piece of webbing on the unpressed

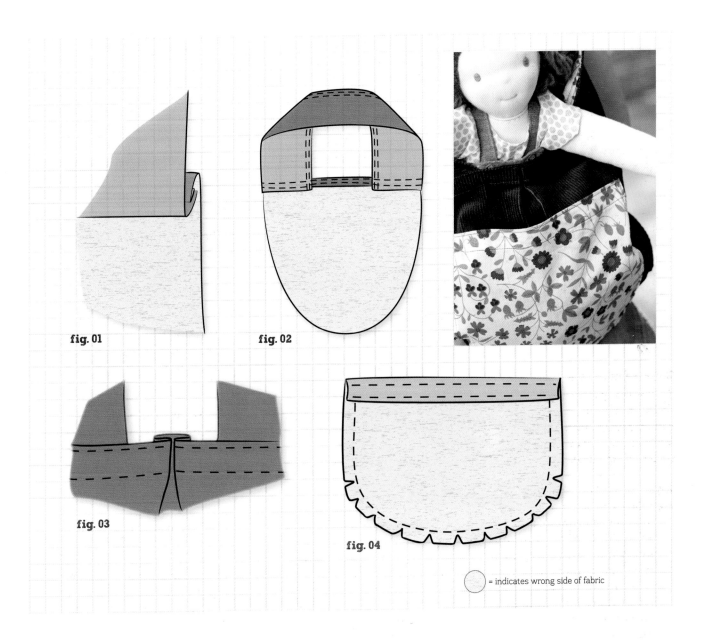

fig. 01

fig. 02

fig. 03

fig. 04

⬭ = indicates wrong side of fabric

short end, right side up, matching the raw edges, with the bulk of the webbing lying on the Strap. Press ½" (1.3 cm) to the wrong side on one short end of a Contrast Strap. Lay the Contrast Strap on the prepared Main Strap, right sides together and raw edges matched, sandwiching the webbing between the layers. Sew both long edges and the

short end with the webbing, leaving the pressed short end open for turning. Clip the corners diagonally.

15 Turn the strap right side out by pulling the fabric through the open short end of the strap and press. Topstitch ¼" (6 mm) from the edge along all four Strap edges.

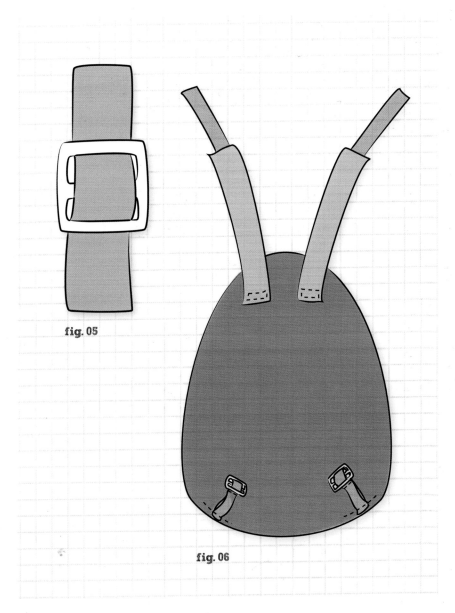

fig. 05

fig. 06

of the webbing as close to the slide adjuster bar as possible. Pin the short edges of the webbing between the notches on the Main fabric side of the Back's lower edge, with the webbing lying on the Back and the raw edges matched. Repeat entire step to make and pin the remaining webbing loop to the Papoose Back. Baste both in place.

19 Align the short Strap ends without webbing with the lower pairs of dots on the Back (**fig. 06**). The Main fabric of the Straps should be facing the Main fabric Back, with the bulk of the Straps lying above the dots. Pin the straps in place and sew a ½" × 2" (1.3 × 5 cm) rectangle through all layers at the base of each Strap, using the dots as guides, securing the straps to the Back.

Finish the Papoose

20 Fold the Straps downward, over the stitched rectangles, and pin them to the center of the Back, away from remaining seams. Pin the assembled Front to the Back, right sides together, with the Pocket, Straps and webbing loops between the layers. Serge the papoose together around the outer edges, or sew a ¼" (6 mm) seam and then finish the seam allowances as one with a zigzag stitch. Turn the papoose right side out.

21 Unpin the straps. Thread the Strap webbing through the slide adjusters as in Step 18, so the Strap webbing lies on top of the webbing loop. Turn ⅜" (1 cm) to the wrong side on each unfinished webbing end and topstitch close to the fold. To keep the webbing from raveling, finish the raw edges with seam sealant.

16 Repeat Steps 14 and 15 from * to make the second strap. Set both straps aside for now.

Prepare the Papoose Back

17 Pin the Main Back to the Contrast Back with wrong sides (interfacing) together. Increase the stitch length on your machine to 4.0–5.0 mm and stitch ¼" (6 mm) from the edge to baste.

18 To make a webbing loop, take one of the remaining 4" (10 cm) pieces of webbing and thread it through a slide adjuster (**fig. 05**). Fold the webbing in half, matching the short ends, and sew across the width

For artists of all ages, the Art Satchel is a studio-on-the-go that allows a child to take along fifteen crayons or pencils, ten markers, a drawing pad, and a flat surface on which to draw (thanks to the Plexiglas inserts). Snap it closed, and your child can carry it by the handles when he's ready to head back inside. He can take the Art Satchel to his "Sit Spot" (see page 101), observe the birds and plants, and draw what he sees—an exercise that will help him come to know the flora and fauna of your neighborhood.

FINISHED SIZE 11¼" × 14¼" (28.5 × 36 cm) when closed.

FABRIC + MATERIALS

- 1½ yd (1.4 m) of 54" (137 cm) wide home decor-weight cotton or cotton/linen blend fabric (Main; *shown:* nature/animal print by Echino)

- ⅜ yd (34.5 cm) of 45" (114.5 cm) wide solid cotton fabric (Contrast)

- 2 sheets of ¼" (6 mm) thick Plexiglas, custom cut to 11" × 14" (28 × 35.5 cm; available for a reasonable price at glass shops)

- One ¾" (19 mm) magnetic snap

- ⅛ yd (11.5 cm) of 20" (51 cm) wide medium-weight fusible interfacing

- Two 1⅛" (28 mm) buttons (*shown:* round wooden buttons)

- Coordinating sewing thread

- 6" (15.5 cm) of coordinating thin elastic cord or two thin elastic hair ties

- Swedish tracing paper or other pattern paper

TOOLS

- Art Satchel pattern in pattern envelope

- Yardstick

- Tailor's chalk or fabric marking pen

- Rotary cutter, quilter's ruler, and self-healing mat (optional)

- Zipper foot for sewing machine

- Handsewing needle

- Loop turner

- Flat-nose pliers (optional; for snap installation)

notes

- ½" (1.3 cm) seam allowances are used unless otherwise noted.

- I like to use Sharps handsewing needles for this project; they are short and easy to maneuver.

Cut the Fabric

1 Trace the Marker Pouch Front pattern piece onto Swedish tracing paper or other pattern paper, transferring all pattern markings, and cut out.

2 Lay the Main fabric, right side up, in a single layer on a flat surface. Plan the arrangement of the pieces listed below to take advantage of the fabric's design; the sample features a large panel print that flows across the exterior, with smaller patterned areas of the fabric used for the interior pieces. As the pieces are cut, mark each with a removable fabric pen or tailor's chalk to avoid confusion during assembly.

3 From the Main fabric, cut:
* Two Body Panels: 15¼" long × 25" wide (38.5 × 63.5 cm); position the print carefully on one panel for the exterior.
* One Crayon Holder: 10¾" long × 23" wide (27.5 × 58.5 cm)
* One Marker Pouch Front from pattern
* One Marker Pouch Flap: 3⅞" long × 7¾" wide (9.8 × 19.5 cm)
* Two Handles: 12" long × 3" wide (30.5 × 7.5 cm)
* One Paper Pad Pocket: 10½" × 10½" (26.5 × 26.5 cm)
* One Tab Closure: 4½" long × 3" wide (11.5 × 7.5 cm)

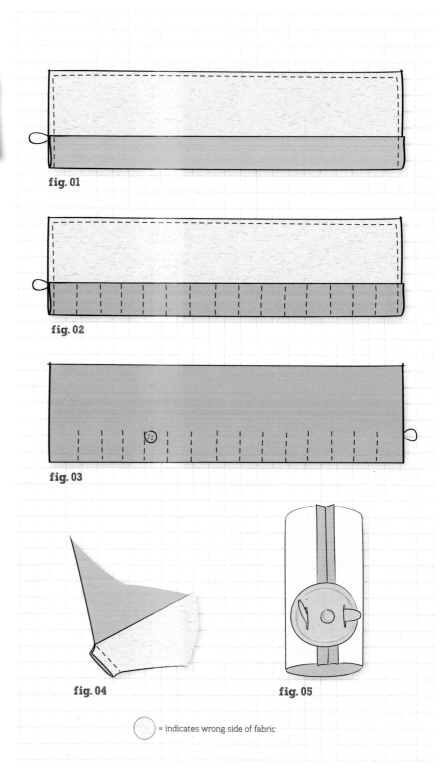

fig. 01

fig. 02

fig. 03

fig. 04

fig. 05

= indicates wrong side of fabric

4 From the Contrast fabric, cut:
* One Crayon Holder: 10¾" long × 23" wide (27.5 × 58.5 cm)
* One Marker Pouch Back: 5" long × 7¾" wide (12.5 × 19.5 cm)
* One Marker Pouch Flap: 3⅞" long × 7¾" wide (9.8 × 19.5 cm)

5 From the fusible interfacing, cut:
* One Tab Closure: 4½" long × 3" wide (11.5 × 7.5 cm)
* One reinforcement: 2" × 2" (5 × 5 cm)

Make the Crayon Holder

6 Cut the elastic in half so you have two equal lengths. Set one piece aside.

7 Fold one piece of elastic in half and baste it to the right side of the Main Crayon Holder, 5½" (14 cm) below the top right corner. Match the elastic and fabric raw edges, with the elastic ends ¼" (6 mm) apart and the bend in the elastic toward the middle of the fabric. Pin the Main and Contrast fabric Crayon Holder pieces right sides together, matching the raw edges. Sew along the entire perimeter, leaving a 3" (7.5 cm) gap for turning along the top long edge and catching the elastic ends in the seam. Trim the corners (page 145) and turn the Crayon Holder right side out. Press flat, with the elastic loop extending from the left short edge when the Contrast lining is on top.

8 With the lining side facing up and the elastic loop on the left, fold 3" (7.5 cm) of the bottom edge to the lining side and pin in place. Edgestitch (page 142) the top and sides as shown in **fig. 01**, securing the fold to form a long pocket and closing the gap in the upper edge.

9 Using a fabric pen or tailor's chalk, draw lines 1½" (3.8 cm) apart from the top of the pocket to the bottom, beginning at one short edge of the Crayon Holder. There should be fourteen lines, each 3" (7.6 cm) long, across the pocket (**fig. 02**).

10 Beginning at the folded bottom edge of the pocket, stitch along each drawn line to the top edge of the pocket and backtack (page 142) to reinforce the pocket opening. There will be fifteen crayon pockets (**fig. 02**). Fold the long top edge down over the pocket openings, lining sides together, so the long edge slightly overlaps the top edge of the pockets. Press the top fold to crease, forming the top flap.

11 With the Main fabric side of the Crayon Holder facing up and the elastic loop to the right, count four crayon pocket seams from the left and attach one button ⅜" (1 cm) to the right of the fourth seam and 3" (7.5 cm) above the bottom folded edge (**fig. 03**). Be careful not to sew the pocket closed as you attach the button. Set aside the Crayon Holder for now.

Make the Marker Pouch

12 Fold the remaining piece of elastic in half as in Step 6 and center it on the bottom edge of the Main fabric Marker Pouch Flap. Match the elastic and fabric raw edges, with the elastic ends ¼" (6 mm) apart and the bend in the elastic toward the middle of the fabric, then baste in place. Pin the Main and Contrast Marker Pouch Flaps right sides together, then sew around the perimeter, leaving a 2" (5 cm) opening for turning in the side opposite the elastic. Clip the corners and turn the flap right side out. Press flat, pressing the seam allowances to the wrong side at the gap. Edgestitch around the entire flap, closing the gap. Set aside.

13 Fold the Marker Pouch Front diagonally, right sides together, matching the notches at one lower corner, and stitch the corner seam from the raw edges to the diagonal fold with a ¼" (6 mm) seam allowance (**fig. 04**). Repeat for the other lower corner.

14 Pin the Marker Pouch Back and Marker Pouch Front, right sides together, along the side and bottom edges of the pouch. Sew, using a ¼" (6 mm) seam allowance. Press the seam open.

15 With the Pouch still inside out, press ¼" (6 mm) to the wrong side around the entire top edge (Main and Contrast). Press another ½" (1.3 cm) to the wrong side and pin in place; edgestitch along the inner fold to secure the hem.

16 With coordinating thread and a handsewing needle, sew the remaining button to the center front of the Marker Pouch, 1½" (3.8 cm) below the top edge. Set the Pouch aside for now.

Make the Drawing Pad Pocket

17 Press ¼" (6 mm) to the wrong side along one edge of the Drawing Pad Pocket. Press another ½" (1.3 cm) to the wrong side along the same edge and pin in place. Edgestitch along the inner fold to complete the hem for the pocket's top edge.

18 Press ½" (1.3 cm) to the wrong side along the other three edges of the Drawing Pad Pocket in preparation for sewing it to the Main Panel Lining in Step 27. Set aside.

Make the Handles + the Tab Closure

19 Fold one of the Handle pieces in half lengthwise with right sides together and sew along the entire 12" (30.5 cm) length using a ¼" (6 mm) seam allowance, forming a tube. Press the seam open, centering it in the middle of the handle. Use a loop turner to turn the tube right side out. Press the tube flat, centering the seam on the back. Edgestitch both long edges of the handle. Repeat entire step to make the other handle. Set both aside.

20 Fuse the interfacing to the wrong side of the Main fabric Tab Closure, following the manufacturer's instructions. Press ¼" (6 mm) to the wrong side along one short edge. Fold the Tab Closure in half lengthwise with right sides together. Sew along the 4½" (11.5 cm) edge, using a ¼" (6 mm) seam allowance, forming a tube. Press the seam open so that it is centered in the middle, as in Step 19.

21 Take one of the metal washers from the magnetic snap and place it on the tube, centered directly over the seam, with the center of the washer ¾" (1.9 cm) below the tube's

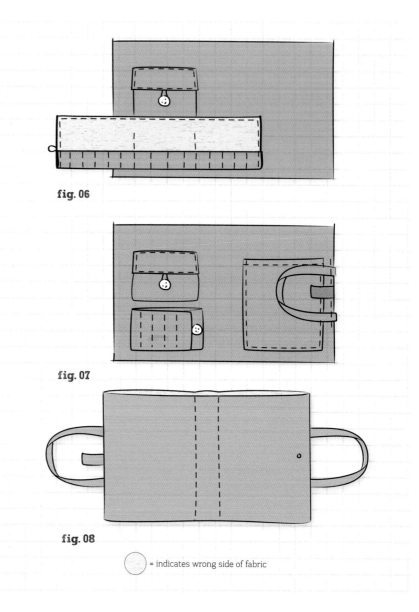

fig. 06

fig. 07

fig. 08

⬤ = indicates wrong side of fabric

pressed short edge. Use a pen or pencil to mark the placement of the two side slits, using the washer as a stencil. Set the washer aside and use a seam ripper or embroidery scissors to cut slits through the back layer of fabric/interfacing only, along the marked lines.

22 Select the male snap with its prongs attached and slip the

prongs through the slits from the right side of the tube (currently the interior as the tube is inside out). Replace the washer over the prongs on the wrong (interfaced) side of the tube and fold the prongs flat toward the outer edges of the snap (**fig. 05** on page 96). Use flat-nose pliers, if necessary, to grasp and flatten the prongs.

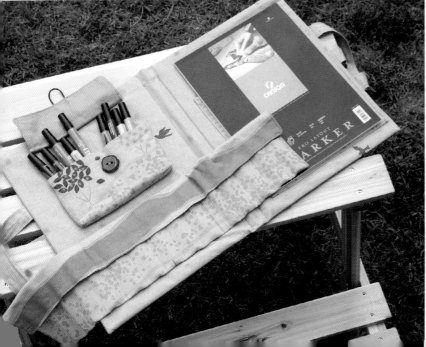

23 Turn the tube right side out and press, keeping the seam centered on the back side of the Tab. Using a zipper foot on the sewing machine, edgestitch around the three finished edges of the Tab Closure.

Assemble the Interior

24 Thread the handsewing needle with thread that matches the Main fabric. Pin the Marker Pouch to the interior Body Panel, 4¼" (11 cm) below the long top edge and 3" (7.5 cm) from the short left edge of the Panel. Pin along the upper edge of the Contrast fabric Marker Pouch Back only and handsew this top edge first, using a blindstitch (page 143) to secure the Contrast fabric pouch to the Body Panel. Once the top edge is attached, pin and stitch the remaining three edges of the pouch, exactly following the seam that joins the Pouch Back to the Pouch Front. The Back will lie flat across the Body Panel, while the front should "poof" out a bit. Secure the thread by taking a few very short stitches in the lining fabric, then knot it off on the wrong side of the Body Panel. With a doubled thread, take a few stitches, one over the other, at the very center of the Pouch's upper edge, joining the Back and Front. Sew through all layers and knot off on the wrong side of the Main Panel lining. These center stitches will keep the markers from shifting inside the pouch.

25 Center the top edge of the Marker Flap (the longer edge that doesn't have the elastic loop) 2¾" (7 cm) above the top edge of the Marker Pouch. Pin in place and use a sewing machine straight stitch to edgestitch the Flap to the Body Panel, following the previous line of stitches.

26 Position the Crayon Holder below the Marker Pouch, 1½" (3.8 cm) above the bottom edge of the Body Panel, aligning the sixth and tenth stitching lines from the left side with the Marker Pouch sides. Pin the Crayon Holder to the Body Panel between the sixth and tenth lines and sew directly over these two lines, extending the stitching 1¾" (4.5 cm) above the pocket edge (**fig. 06** on page 98). The folded lower edge of the Crayon Holder is not attached to the Body Panel.

27 Place the prepared Drawing Pad Pocket right side up on the Body Panel 1½" (3.8 cm) above the bottom of the Body Panel and 1" (2.5 cm) from the Body Panel's right edge. Be sure the hemmed Pocket edge is toward the top of the Body Panel. Edgestitch the pocket to the Body Panel along the side and lower edges.

Assemble the Satchel

28 Pin one end of a prepared Handle to the right edge of the interior Body Panel, 4½" (11.5 cm) below the Panel's upper edge, matching the raw edges. The center seam of the Handle should be facing the right side of the interior Body Panel. Pin the other end of the same Handle 4½" (11.5 cm) above the Body Panel's lower edge, making sure the Handle is not twisted. Baste ⅜" (1 cm) from the raw edges (see **fig. 07** on page 98). Repeat to attach the remaining Handle to the left edge of the interior Body Panel.

29 Center the Tab Closure between the ends of the Handle along the Body Panel's right edge (nearest the Drawing Pad Pocket), with the snap component facing down (toward the Body Panel) and the raw edges aligned. Baste ⅜" (1 cm) from the edge (**fig. 07** on page 98).

30 Fuse a 2" × 2" (5 × 5 cm) square of fusible interfacing to the wrong side of the exterior Body Panel, 2½" (6.5 cm) from the left edge and 7⅝" (19.3 cm) from both the upper and lower edges. Attach the female component of the magnetic snap to the right side of the fabric, centering it on the interfaced fabric and referring to Steps 21 and 22.

31 Place the exterior and interior Body Panels right sides together with raw edges aligned. Make sure that the Handles and Tab Closure are properly sandwiched between the layers. Pin together along the side and lower edges, leaving the entire top edge open for turning. Sew the three sides and then clip the corners. Turn the satchel right side out and press the seam flat, keeping the iron away from the dimensional pockets. Press ⅜" (1 cm) to the wrong side along the entire upper edge of the satchel.

32 Measure and use a removable fabric pen or tailor's chalk to mark a line 11½" (29 cm) from each short end of the satchel, running from the upper edge to the lower edge (**fig. 08** on page 98), and dividing the satchel in the center. Sew along both lines all the way from the lower edge to the upper edge, catching the pressed upper edges in the seams (**fig. 08**).

33 Insert the custom-cut Plexiglas sheets into the pockets just formed; the fit will be snug. Carefully pull the pressed edge of the exterior Body Panel over the top of each Plexiglas sheet, concealing the Plexiglas at the top of the satchel. Using a handsewing needle and thread, slip-stitch (page 143) the entire top edge closed.

nature as teacher

Spending time outside, in nature, is such an important experience for children. I've outlined a few suggestions below to get you started on setting up a backyard that's friendly for nature exploration. You'll soon see that cultivating an appreciation for nature in your children is fun and easy!

• Plant whatever native foliage you can to attract local birds and butterflies, as well as planting herbs and other plants that are useful for kitchen and medicinal purposes. Check your local library for books on the subject. In front of each plant place a little marker on which you write the plant's name and special characteristics.

• Keep a small piece of plywood or a larger, movable rock on the ground. Occasionally lift it up to discover what insects have moved in!

• Make a rustic sandbox by surrounding a space with large logs (and digging a trench to secure the lower 5 to 6 inches [12.5–15 cm] of the logs) and then filling the contained area with sand.

• Choose an area in the yard where you can leave a pile of dirt and provide child-sized digging tools. In rain, this will become a mud puddle—all the more fun!

• Encourage your child to find a special "Sit Spot" where he or she can sit quietly for a few minutes each day (and model the behavior yourself by finding your own Sit Spot). The idea is to become familiar with one small space, observing insects, birds, and animals that pass nearby. It should be a special place, and eventually, if you are quiet and still enough, the animals will grow accustomed to your presence, perhaps revealing themselves to you in new ways!

For nature connection, we use only one golden rule: *notice everything.*

—Evan McGown, from *Coyote's Guide to Connecting with Nature*

naturalist's
scavenger hunt bag

Every budding naturalist needs proper gear—a sun hat, perhaps binoculars, and a bag in which to gather specimens. The Naturalist's Scavenger Hunt Bag provides a child-friendly way to store found objects, because it is fastener-free and adjustable. Attach a set of scavenger hunt cards to the grommet on the strap and fill up the pocket with mini clothespins (see Resources on page 158). Once the child finds one of the objects in her set, show her how to mark it as "found" with a mini clothespin.

FINISHED SIZE 10" wide × 7½" high (not including strap) × 2" deep (25.5 × 19 × 5 cm).

FABRIC + MATERIALS

- ⅝ yd (57 cm) 45" (114.5 cm) wide medium- to heavyweight cotton for lining and trim (Main; *shown:* circle and ladybug print)

- ⅝ yd (57 cm) 45" (114.5 cm) wide medium- to heavyweight cotton for shell (Contrast; *shown:* brown).

- Coordinating sewing thread

- Swedish tracing paper or other pattern paper

- 1 extra large eyelet (⁷⁄₁₆" [1.1 cm]) and eyelet installation tool (can usually be bought together as a kit; see Notes)

- 5¼" (13.5 cm) length of ¾" (2 cm) wide Velcro

- 3" (7.5 cm) length of ½" (1.3 cm) wide coordinating grosgrain ribbon

TOOLS

- Scavenger Hunt Bag pattern in pattern envelope

- Hammer for applying eyelet

- Rotary cutter, quilter's ruler, and self-healing mat (optional for cutting)

notes

- ½" (1.3 cm) seam allowances are used unless otherwise noted.

- Remember to wash, dry, and press fabrics before beginning.

- Eyelets/grommets and the installation tool can usually be found as a kit. However, if you are unable to find the kit, you can buy the tool separately (try Dritz #661T or #660). You'll also need a hammer and a hard flat surface for hammering; be sure to use a sturdy surface that won't be damaged by the hammer.

Cut the Fabric

1 Trace the pattern pieces onto Swedish tracing paper or other pattern paper, transferring all pattern markings, and cut out.

2 From the Main fabric, cut:
* Two Front/Back (fold fabric to cut both of these at once, then unfold to cut the remaining pieces)
* One Clothespin Pocket
* One Gusset: 27" × 3" (68.5 × 7.5 cm)
* One Long Strap: 24¾" × 3" (63 × 7.5 cm)
* One Adjustable Strap 12¾" × 3" (32 × 7.5 cm)
* One Top Flap: 11" × 7" (28 × 18 cm)

3 Repeat Step 2 with the Contrast fabric.

Sew the Pocket

4 Press ¼" (6 mm) to the wrong side along the straight edge of each Pocket piece. Pin the Main and Contrast fabric Pocket pieces right sides together and sew with a ¼" (6 mm) seam allowance along the curved bottom edge. Clip the seam allowances (page 145) along the curve, turn the pocket right side out, and press flat. Topstitch (page 142) ⅛" (3 mm) from the straight edge, to close it and finish the pocket.

5 Pin the assembled pocket, Main fabric side up, to the right side of the Contrast Front, centering the pocket 2" (5 cm) below the straight upper edge of the Front. Topstitch ⅛" (3 mm) from the Pocket's curved edge to attach it to the Front. Set aside the Front for now.

Prepare the Top Flap + Straps

6 Pin the Main and Contrast fabric Top Flaps right sides together. Sew along three sides, leaving one of the long sides open for turning. Clip the corners (page 145) and turn the Flap right side out. Press flat. Topstitch ¼" (6 mm) and ½" (1.3 cm) from each seamed edge, pivoting at the corners to form neat right angles in the topstitching. Set aside the Top Flap.

7 Place the piece of grosgrain ribbon on the right side of the Main fabric Long Strap, ⅝" (1.5 cm) from one short end (**fig. 01**). Baste (page 142) the ribbon ends to the fabric ¼" (6 mm) from the raw edges. Pin the Main and Contrast Long Straps, right sides together, and sew along three sides, leaving the short edge farthest from the ribbon open for turning. The ribbon is positioned just ⅛" (3 mm) from the seamline, so be careful not to catch the longer edge of the ribbon in the seam! Clip the corners and turn the Strap right side out. Press flat, then topstitch ¼" (6 mm) from each long edge,

beginning your stitching beside the ribbon; don't narrow the ribbon loop by topstitching across it. Set aside.

8 Separate the Velcro. Fold the Contrast fabric Adjustable Strap in half, widthwise, and crease lightly. Open the fabric, right side up, and center the Velcro sections on the fabric right side, with the Velcro short ends meeting at the center crease. Edgestitch (page 142) all edges of the fastener (**fig. 02**).

9 Pin the Main and Contrast Adjustable Straps right sides together, sandwiching the Velcro between the layers. Sew along three sides of the strap, leaving the short edge nearest the hook portion of the Velcro open for turning. Clip the corners, turn right side out, and press flat. Topstitch ¼" (6 mm) from the edge along the three finished sides.

10 Follow the manufacturer's instructions to attach the eyelet, centered on the Main fabric side, ¾" (2 cm) from the finished short end of the Adjustable Strap.

11 Thread the eyelet end of the Adjustable Strap through the ribbon on the Long Strap with the Velcro meeting inside the fold. Fold down the adjustable strap and fasten, leaving at least 2" (5 cm) of the Velcro hooks visible to keep the eyelet away from the seams during assembly. Set aside the assembled Strap.

Sew the Gusset to the Front + Back

12 Fold the Contrast Gusset in half widthwise to find the center. Mark both seam allowances at the center fold. Pin the Contrast Gusset to the curved edge of one of the Main

Front/Back Panels, right sides together, matching the Panel's center notch to the mark at the Gusset center. Pin from the center outward, toward the top edges (**fig. 03**). Use a lot of pins as you ease (page 142) the Gusset along the bag curves.

13 Sew the Gusset to the Panel, stitching slowly as you arrive at the curves and using your fingers to smooth the fabric as you go to avoid tucks and gathers in the seam.

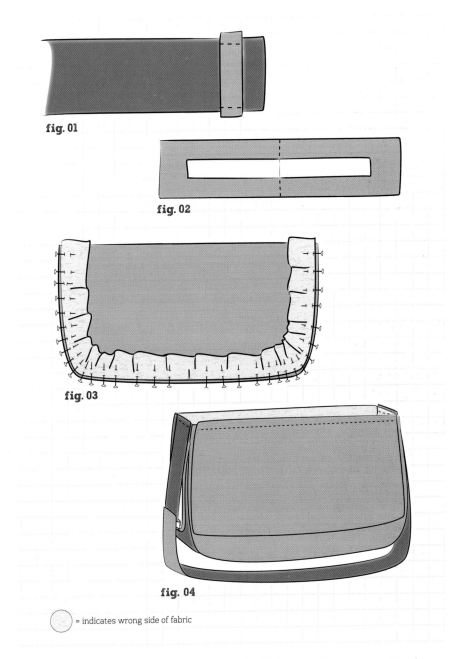

fig. 01

fig. 02

fig. 03

fig. 04

⬤ = indicates wrong side of fabric

14 Repeat Steps 12 and 13 to attach the second Main Front/Back Panel to the other long side of the Contrast Gusset, this time leaving a 4" (10 cm) opening in the seam along the bottom for turning. Clip the curves along both Gusset seams and press the seam allowances open. This is the bag lining.

15 To make the bag shell, repeat Steps 12 and 13 with the Contrast Front/Back Panels and the Main Gusset, without leaving a gap for turning. Turn the bag shell right side out.

Assemble + Finish the Bag

16 Pin the Top Flap to the unfinished edge of the bag shell, pinning to the side without the pocket. Align the Top Flap and shell bag raw edges and position the Main fabric side of the Flap against the right side of the shell.

17 Pin one end of the assembled strap to the shell, with the fastener lying against the right side of the gusset to the left of the pinned Flap. Pin the other end of the strap to the shell with the Main fabric, against the right side of the gusset to the right of the flap. Center the strap ends over the gusset at each side, with their raw edges matched. Ensure that the strap is not twisted, then baste each strap end and the top flap to the bag, ¼" (6 mm) from the raw edges (**fig. 04** on page 105).

18 With the lining wrong side out and the shell right side out, place the shell inside the lining, right sides together, aligning the gussets and matching the raw edges. Make sure that the strap and the top flap are sandwiched between the layers, then pin together along the top edge. Stitch slowly and carefully along the entire top of the bag.

19 Pull the shell through the gap in the lining bag's bottom seam and turn the bag right side out. Tuck in the seam allowances along the opening and slip-stitch (page 142) closed. Arrange the lining inside the shell and press the top edge. Topstitch around the top edge of the bag, ¼" (6 mm) from the edge.

scavenger hunt cards

Make a set of scavenger hunt cards using one of the following options:

● Cut images out of magazines and paste them onto card stock, using precut cards or cutting the card stock to the desired dimensions.

● Print images from the computer directly onto card stock.

● Print your own photos onto business cards at home or have them professionally made for a more polished look.

Punch a hole near one short end of each card. Thread a set of twenty cards onto a 10" (25.5 cm) length of hemp string and tie the ends of the string together in a knot. Thread the knotted end of the card set through the eyelet on the bag, then open up the string and pull the cards through the string loop.

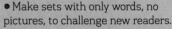
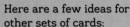

Here are a few ideas for other sets of cards:

● Make sets with only words, no pictures, to challenge new readers.

● For the more advanced reader, write a description of the object on the card instead of the name itself. For example: *I grow in clumps or mats in damp or shady locations. I don't have flowers or seeds, but I am a brilliant green color. What am I?* (Answer: *moss.*)

● Make I Spy sets. These sets don't require the child to add the object to his bag. Instead, equip him with a set of binoculars and a magnifying glass tucked away in his bag. Once he sees an object on one of his cards, such as a Cardinal or a pine tree, he can mark it off with a mini clothespin.

hideaway
play tent

Children love to have a place in which to hide, construct their own little worlds, create their own rules, and enjoy a bit of solitude. The Hideaway Play Tent provides just that—a refuge from wide-open spaces. Pitch the tent in a corner of your yard, underneath a tree, or bring it into the living room during a rainy day. It's perfectly sized for two small children or one older child and could also be used as a shelter for bird-watching. The circular window in the back opens and closes with Velcro, so the tent inhabitant can peep out, observing nature in action.

FINISHED SIZE 35" wide × 35" deep × 54" high (89 × 89 × 137 cm)

FABRIC + MATERIALS

- 3¼ yd (3 m) of 54" (137 cm) wide cotton canvas fabric for tent (Main)

- 1⅜ yd (1.3 m) of 54" (137 cm) wide home decor–weight fabric for the rod casings and binding (Contrast)

- Coordinating sewing thread

- 6" (15 cm) length of ¾" (2 cm) wide Velcro

- Swedish tracing paper or other pattern paper (for making your own pattern; see page 110)

- 1½ yd (137 cm) length of twine or other strong, thin cord for tying together bamboo rods

- Masking tape

TOOLS

- Tent Window template in pattern envelope

- Yardstick (optional)

- Jeans/denim or other sharp sewing machine needle (size 110/18)

- Four bamboo rods, each 5' long × 1" in diameter (1.5 m × 2.5 cm; available at many nursery/garden shops)

- Rotary cutter, quilter's ruler, and self-healing mat (optional for cutting)

- Drill and a ⁹⁄₆₄ drill bit (or a drill bit of appropriate diameter for your twine or cord)

notes

- ½" (1.3 cm) seam allowances are used unless otherwise noted.

- After cutting, mark the right side of each piece with a small piece of masking tape to avoid confusion during assembly.

Make the Pattern + Cut the Fabric

*Refer to **fig. 01** for assistance with the following steps.*

1 Cut a piece of Swedish tracing paper or other pattern paper that is at least 47" × 40" (119.5 × 101.5 cm). Tape sections of paper together, if necessary, to reach the correct size. Fold the paper in half lengthwise, forming a doubled piece measuring at least 47" × 20" (119.5 × 51 cm).

2 Draw a line 18¾" (47.5 cm) long perpendicular to and starting at the fold and about 1" (2.5 cm) from the bottom edge of the paper. Label the end of the line opposite the fold as **A**.

3 Measure along the fold and mark 44¼" (112.5 cm) above the line just drawn. Draw a line 2¼" (5.5 cm) long, perpendicular to the fold and beginning at the mark. Label the end of this line opposite the fold as **B**.

4 Use a yardstick or other straightedge to draw a line connecting **A** and **B**. Cut out the pattern piece through both layers but do not cut the folded edge. Unfold to reveal a trapezoidal pattern piece; label this Tent Panel. Use a straightedge to draw a line along the foldline, perpendicular to the top and bottom edges; mark as the grainline.

5 Measure 17¾" (45 cm) from the top (short edge) along the foldline/grainline and mark. Use a straightedge to draw a line across the pattern, parallel to the top edge (**fig. 01**, dashed line). Mark this line as the cutting line for the Door Panel Top, but do not cut the pattern.

6 Draw a line 1" (2.5 cm) above the Door Panel Top cutting line. Label it as the Door Flap cutting line (**fig. 01**, dotted line). The overlap between the cutting lines is seam allowance (again, do not cut the pattern).

7 Cut or assemble another piece of pattern paper measuring at least 30" × 21" (76 × 53.5 cm). Fold the Tent Panel pattern piece in half, lengthwise, along the original foldline. Lay the new piece of pattern paper over the Tent Panel pattern and trace the lower portion, from the bottom edge to the Door Flap cutting line, tracing the fold as one edge of the new pattern. Label this piece Door Flap and mark the grainline parallel to the transferred foldline.

8 Cut or assemble another piece of pattern paper measuring at least 20" × 20" (51 × 51 cm). Unfold the Tent Panel pattern piece and lay the new piece of pattern paper over the Tent Panel pattern. Trace the upper portion, from the short upper edge to the Door Panel Top cutting line. Label this piece as the Door Panel Top, transferring the grainline from the Panel pattern.

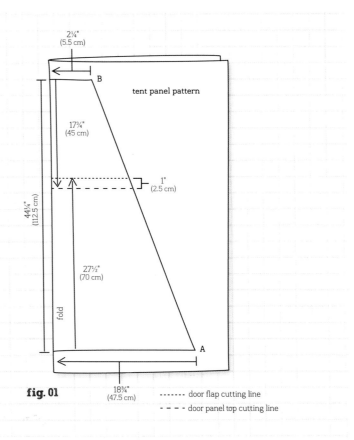

fig. 01

2¼" (5.5 cm)

17¾" (45 cm)

1" (2.5 cm)

44¼" (112.5 cm)

27½" (70 cm)

fold

18¾" (47.5 cm)

tent panel pattern

B

A

········· door flap cutting line

- - - - door panel top cutting line

9 Trace the Tent Window template from the pattern insert onto Swedish tracing paper or other pattern paper and cut out.

10 Cut the following pattern pieces from the Main fabric, right side up and partially folded, as shown in the layout diagram on page 155:
*Three Tent Panels
*Two Door Flaps (cut one, cut one reverse)
*Two Door Panel Tops

11 From the Contrast fabric, right side up, cut:
* Four Rod Casings: 48" × 3" (122 × 7.5 cm)
*Three Binding strips: 40" × 3" (76 × 7.5 cm) cut on the bias (refer to the instructions under bias binding on page 144 for assistance with cutting bias strips); follow the instructions under Double-Fold Binding on page 144 to join the strips and prepare continuous bias binding
*Two Door Side Bindings: 30" × 3" (76 × 7.5 cm) on the straight grain; follow the instructions under Double-Fold Binding; prepare each strip separately
*One Window Tab: 3" × 3¾" (7.5 × 9.5 cm)

Make the Window

12 Center the Window template on one Tent Panel, 15¾" (40 cm) above the wide bottom edge of the Panel. Trace around the template with a fabric marker or tailor's chalk, then use a sharp pair of scissors to make a slit along the line. Continue cutting along the line, creating a circular hole in the Panel. Reserve the cutout circle of fabric to use as the window shutter.

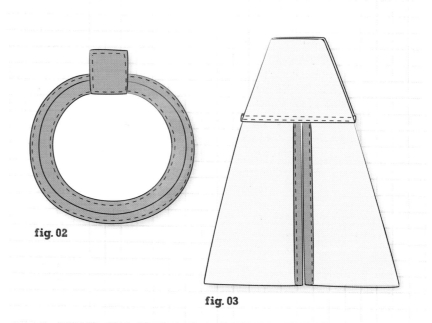

fig. 02

fig. 03

13 Bind the outer edge of the window shutter by slipping the circle's edge, right side up, into the binding. The wider side of the binding should be on the wrong side of the circle with the circle raw edge completely into the binding's center crease. Edgestitch (page 142) along the inner edge of the binding, being sure to catch the binding's back edge as well. When about 3" (7.6 cm) of the edge remains to be bound, cut off the excess binding ¾" (2 cm) beyond the leading edge of the binding. Fold ⅜" (1 cm) to the wrong side along the trailing end of the binding, then stitch the remaining binding to the shutter circle, overlapping the unfinished leading edge of the binding. Press the bound circle flat and set aside.

14 Bind the circular window opening in the Panel as in Step 13, beginning at the center top of the opening. Press the circle and binding flat.

15 Press ½" (1.3 cm) to the wrong side along all four edges of the Window Tab. Lay the window Tent Panel, right side up, on a flat surface and position the window shutter, right side up, inside the opening, aligning the binding ends at the top of the opening so both junctures can be concealed under the Window Tab. Lay the Window Tab over the bindings, aligning its lower edge with the inside edge of the shutter's binding. Make sure the Tab is centered on the Panel with its upper edge parallel to the Panel's upper edge to avoid hanging the shutter crookedly. Pin in place and edgestitch around all four edges of the Tab as shown in **fig. 02**.

16 Cut a 2" (5 cm) length of Velcro and separate the halves. Center the loop side of the Velcro vertically

on the wrong side of the window Tent Panel, 6½" (16.5 cm) above the window opening. Edgestitch around all four edges of the Velcro to secure it. Repeat to attach the hook portion of the Velcro to the wrong side of the window shutter, centering it ¼" (6 mm) from the outer bound edge, overlapping the binding. Set aside the window panel for now.

Assemble the Door Panel

17 Use one length of the straight-grain binding (made in Step 11) to bind the vertical (not slanted) edge of one Door Flap. Position the Door Flap's raw edge in the binding fold, with the wider binding edge on the wrong side. Pin the binding in place, then edgestitch the binding along the inner edges, stitching through all layers. Check often to ensure that the bottom edge of the binding (on the wrong side of the Door) is also caught in the seam. Trim the excess binding even with the upper and lower Door Flap edges. Repeat to attach the remaining binding to the second Door Flap.

18 Lay the Door Flaps on one Door Panel Top, right sides together, matching the raw edges at the top of the Flaps to the bottom edge of the Door Panel Top. The bound edges of the Flaps should meet at the center of the Door Panel Top without overlapping. Pin the pieces together. Position the right side of the second Door Panel Top against the wrong side of the Door Flaps, matching the raw edges with the first Door Panel Top, and pin. Sew the seam through all layers. Press the Door Flaps away from the Door Panel Tops. Topstitch (page 142) ⅛" (3 mm) and ⅜" (1 cm) from the seam on the Door Panel Top through all layers (**fig. 03**).

Assemble the Tent

You will be sewing the panels with their wrong sides together. This can be counterintuitive, but I find it helpful to keep in mind that the inside of the tent will look just as "finished" as the outside of the tent. The seams you create on the outside (right side) of the tent will eventually be hidden by the Rod Casings.

19 Pin the Door Panel to one of the plain Tent Panels (no window), wrong sides together, aligning one long angled edge. Sew the edges and press the seam open.

20 Pin the remaining angled edge of the plain Tent Panel to one edge of the Window Panel. Sew and press as before (**fig. 04**). Sew the remaining plain Tent Panel to the other side of the Window Panel and press the seam open as before.

21 Sew the remaining sides of the Door Panel and the plain Tent Panel together and press the seam open as before.

22 To facilitate hemming the lower edge, use a large cup or small plate to round the corners where the panels meet at the side seams (**fig. 05**). Trace the cup or plate edge at each corner with a fabric marking pen or tailor's chalk and then trim the fabric along the traced line.

23 Press ¼" (6 mm) to the wrong side along the entire lower edge. Press an additional ½" (1.3 cm) to the wrong side and pin, easing in (page 142) the extra fullness. Edgestitch along the inner fold to secure the hem.

24 Sew the last strip of bias binding to the top raw edge of the tent, using the same technique as in Step 13.

Attach the Rod Casings

25 Press ½" (1.3 cm) to the wrong side on both short ends of a Rod Casing and stitch ⅜" (1 cm) from each pressed edge.

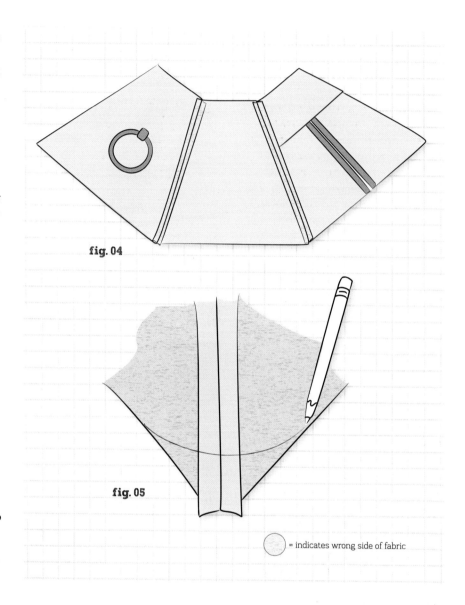

fig. 04

fig. 05

= indicates wrong side of fabric

26 Press ⅜" (1 cm) to the wrong side along both long edges. Pin the Casing to the tent right side, centered on one exposed, pressed-open seam. Beginning at the top and working toward the bottom, pin the Casing long edges to the tent, being careful to catch only one layer of canvas and not the other side of the tent! Pin perpendicular to the pressed long casing edges. If the Casing doesn't fit the tent accurately, remove the hem at one short end of the casing, adjust, sew the corrected hem, then put in the final pins.

27 Beginning at the bottom of the tent, edgestitch each long casing edge, leaving the hemmed top and bottom ends open.

28 Repeat Steps 25–27 to attach the remaining three Casings to the tent.

29 Cut the remaining Velcro into two pieces and separate the hook and loop portions. Sew one hook section to the exterior of each plain Tent Panel, 18" (46 cm) above the lower edge, beside and parallel to the casing between the plain and Door Panels.

30 Sew one loop section to each Door Flap exterior, 12" (30.5 cm) above the lower edge, overlapping the flap binding but parallel to the casing. Use these fasteners to keep the Door Flaps open.

Prepare the Bamboo Poles + Finish the Tent

31 Drill a hole through each bamboo pole, 7½" (19 cm) from the top end of the pole; the top of the bamboo should have a smaller diameter than the bottom. Choose a drill bit that produces the correct size hole for your twine or cord.

32 Insert a bamboo pole through each of the casings, with the narrower top of the bamboo at the top of the tent. Thread the twine through each of the holes and arrange them so that the tent can open and close with ease. Tie the string together tightly but allowing enough slack for the bamboo poles to shift as the tent is opened and closed. Knot the twine securely and trim the excess.

CHAPTER FIVE

goodnight, sleep tight

When you're a kid, life is too fun to go to sleep! Every day offers such a multitude of interesting experiences and learning opportunities that the word "bedtime" often elicits groans. Unfortunately for them, we adults know that sufficient sleep is essential to their growth and development. When sleep is neglected, the following day becomes a chore, plus it makes kids more susceptible to illness and less capable of integrating new learning experiences.

A predictable daily rhythm, which naturally flows into a relaxing bedtime routine, generally makes bedtime a more pleasant experience for all. In our house, the preparation for bedtime actually begins in the morning! In our son's room, we keep a tote bag, which we call his "bedtime bag" (I use the Funny Animals Children's Tote from my first book, *Sew Liberated: 20 Stylish Projects for the Modern Sewist*). The bag is prepared in the morning and contains his comfy pajamas, which I make using the Envelope Tees (page 8) and the Sleeping Johns (page 118) patterns. We also add his Kitty Lovey Puppet (page 128) to the tote, and then I ask my son to choose a bedtime book to add to the tote as well. If you have a younger child, try adding the Baby Sleep Sack (page 122) and anything else you may need for putting your child to bed. Having the bedtime bag ready and waiting for bedtime helps so much in creating a peaceful evening in our home.

sleeping johns (or everyday leggings)

There's nothing better than climbing into a warm bed in handmade pajamas. Pajamas represent the ultimate in comfort-wear, especially for children. The key to comfy, snug-fitting pajamas is the right fabric. Use a knit fabric with 90 percent cotton, 10 percent spandex content. NearSea Naturals (see Resources on page 158) has a nice selection of organic knit blends. Make up several pairs in different colors and then couple each one with a Crossover Tee (page 24) for a cozy, comfy pajama set.

FINISHED SIZE 2T (3T, 4T, 5) is 19 (21, 23¼, 25½)" (48.5 [53.5, 59, 65] cm) long at the side seam. See the Size Chart on page 145 for more fit information. Sleeping Johns shown are size 5.

FABRIC + MATERIALS

⬧ ¾ (¾, ⅞, ⅞) yd (69 [69, 80, 80] cm) 60" (152.5 cm) wide cotton/spandex blend knit (shown: 90% cotton, 10% spandex)

⬧ Coordinating polyester or polyester-blend sewing thread

⬧ Swedish tracing paper or other pattern paper

⬧ 17 (18, 19, 20)" (43 [45.5, 48.5, 51] cm) of 1" (2.5 cm) wide non-roll elastic for waistband

TOOLS

⬧ Sleeping Johns pattern in pattern envelope

⬧ Ballpoint or stretch sewing machine needle

⬧ Fine ballpoint pins

notes

- All seam allowances are ¼" (6 mm) unless otherwise indicated.

- Remember to wash, dry, and press all fabric before beginning. Take care not to stretch the knit fabrics when pressing and cutting out the pieces.

- See Working with Knits on page 139 for information about the best stitches for seams in knit fabrics.

- Be sure to use the ballpoint or stretch needle on your machine for the entire project, as you will be sewing on knit fabric.

- If you find it difficult to distinguish the right and wrong sides of the fabric, be sure to mark the wrong side of each piece with tailor's chalk or a fabric marker to avoid confusion.

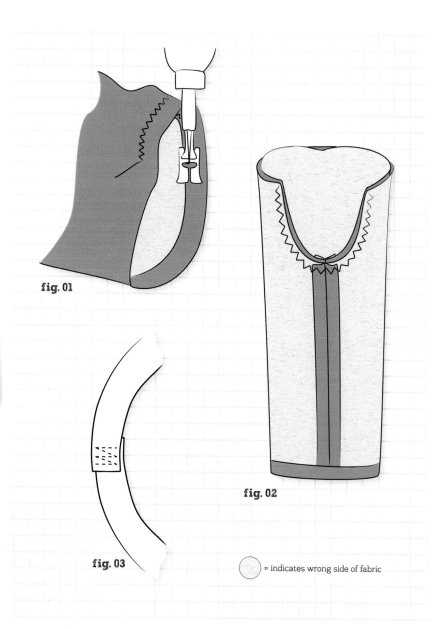

fig. 01

fig. 02

fig. 03

⬭ = indicates wrong side of fabric

Cut the Fabric

1 Trace the pattern onto Swedish tracing paper or other pattern paper, transferring all pattern markings, and cut out. Fold the fabric in half with right sides together, referring to the layout diagram on page 156. Cut two Legs (the fabric is doubled so you will be cutting both pieces at once).

Assemble the Pants

2 Fold one Leg in half lengthwise with right sides together, matching the inseam raw edges. Sew with a stretch stitch or serge together. Press the seam to one side. Repeat to sew the remaining Leg, pressing the seam to the opposite side to reduce bulk when the legs are joined.

3 Turn the pant legs right side out. Press 1" (2.5 cm) toward the wrong side along the bottom edge of each.

Use a stretch stitch or a wide zigzag stitch to hem the pants, topstitching ¾" (1.9 cm) from the fold. If you have a cover stitch machine, use it to complete the hems. You may prefer to sew with the presser foot inside the pant leg, keeping the stitches parallel to and ¼" (6 mm) away from the raw edge (**fig. 01**).

4 Turn one leg right side out and slip it inside the other leg (still inside out). Match the inseams and notches and pin along the crotch seam. Sew the crotch seam with a stretch stitch or serge together (**fig. 02**). Turn the pants right side out and press the crotch seam to one side.

Make the Casing + Sew in the Elastic

5 Check the elastic measurement against the child's waist for a comfortable fit, adjusting the elastic length as necessary. The application method below will prevent the elastic from fully recovering its original length, so it may be necessary to start with a slightly shorter length of elastic; stretch and release the elastic before measuring it around the child's waist. Overlap the ends of the elastic by about ½" (1.3 cm) and stitch together securely by stitching back and forth a few times in a zigzag pattern (**fig. 03**).

6 Press 1⅛" (2.9 cm) to the wrong side along the waist edge of the leggings.

7 Place the elastic circle over the wrong side of the leggings at the

:: tips

• Sleeping Johns also make fabulous everyday leggings for girls! For a super-snazzy pair, cut the pant legs in two different colors—bicolor legs look so fun and cheery under skirts and tunics.

• Try making the leggings in differing lengths for cropped pants or shorts. Simply measure the desired length and add 1" (2.5 cm) for the hems.

• To distinguish pant front and back for children learning to dress themselves, tuck a small loop of ribbon into the casing stitches at the center back.

waist with the elastic seam at the center back, tucking the elastic into the waistline fold. Align the fabric raw edge with the lower edge of the elastic, adjusting the fold if necessary, and pin at the sides and seamlines. The elastic should be slightly smaller in circumference than the waistband fabric; be sure to distribute the waistband fabric evenly around the elastic.

8 With a zigzag stitch or stretch stitch (about 6.0 mm wide), sew along the lower edge of the waistband through the elastic, catching the raw edge in the stitches. Some machines offer multi-step zigzag stitches designed especially for attaching elastic, and those are a good choice if available. Stretch the elastic as you sew so it is evenly distributed between pins. I find it helpful to hold the elastic taut on both sides of the presser foot (before and behind the foot) while sewing, helping to feed the fabric through the machine. Be careful not to stretch too much, as that can interfere with the feed dog and create uneven stitches.

Sewing through the elastic will keep the waistband from twisting uncomfortably, as it has a tendency to do within a standard waistband casing. Easy as pie—you're done!

winding down + tucking in

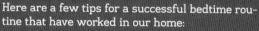

Here are a few tips for a successful bedtime routine that have worked in our home:

• After dinner, we have family music time. Both my husband and I play the guitar, and our son Finn bops along, singing, clapping, playing the drums, or shaking a percussion instrument. We sing a few songs, which helps to get the sillies out—a last burst of energy before we start winding down.

• After family music time, we put on some soft classical music while Finn takes a bath. The evening bath ritual is a wonderful touchstone moment for Finn, because he knows to always expect a pleasant time with just his Daddy. They like to sing songs about water and bathing while Finn is in the tub.

• Following bath time is the teeth brushing song (from Raffi, see Resources) and changing into pajamas and then tucking in.

• Some children respond better to listening to a short story told by Mama or Daddy than to a story from a book. Telling a story to a child makes a personal connection and provides an opportunity to enrich your family's oral heritage.

• Light a candle together, have a moment of silence or recite a verse, and have your child blow out the flame, signaling the transition to sleep.

baby
sleep sack

A twist on the Envelope Tee (page 8), the Baby Sleep Sack provides a soft, no-fuss pajama option. The envelope neckline makes it easy to put on, and the elasticized hem keeps kicking legs warm and covered all night long. The hem also allows for easy diaper changes, eliminating fussy snaps and fasteners that can be difficult to deal with during those groggy middle-of-the-night diaper changes. The Baby Sleep Sack is a must-have for the first twelve months, and it makes the perfect addition to a baby shower gift basket.

FINISHED SIZE 0–6 months (6–12 months) is 19½ (21½)" (49.5 [54.4] cm) at center back. See the Size Chart on page 145 for more fit information. Sleep Sack shown is size 0–6 months.

FABRIC + MATERIALS

- ¾ (⅞) yd (69 [80] cm) of 60" (152.5 cm) wide cotton inter-lock knit (Main)
- ⅛ yd (11.5 cm) of 45–60" (114.5–152.5 cm) wide lightweight cotton rib knit (Contrast)
- Coordinating sewing thread
- 15" (38 cm) length of ½" (1.3 cm) wide non-roll elastic

TOOLS

- Baby Sleep Sack pattern in pattern envelope
- Swedish tracing paper or other pattern paper
- Ballpoint or stretch sewing machine needle
- Fine ballpoint pins
- Rotary cutter, quilter's ruler, and self-healing mat (optional for cutting)
- Safety pin

notes

- ¼" (6 mm) seam allowances are used unless otherwise noted.

- Remember to wash, dry, and press all fabric before beginning. Take care not to stretch the knit fabrics when pressing and cutting out the pieces.

- See Working with Knits on page 139 for information about the best stitches for seams in knit fabrics.

- Be sure to use the ballpoint or stretch needle on your machine for the entire project, as you will be sewing on knit fabric.

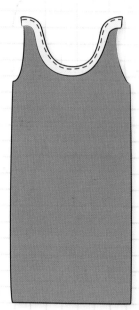

fig. 01

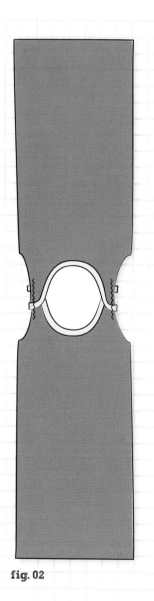

fig. 02

Cut the Fabric

1 Use Swedish tracing paper or other pattern paper to trace the pattern templates from the insert in the back of the book; be sure to transfer all markings and then cut out. Refer to the cutting layout on page 157 for assistance.

2 From the Main fabric, cut:
* One Front on the fold
* One Back on the fold
* Two Sleeves (cut 1, cut 1 reverse); if you'd prefer a short sleeve, use the Envelope Tee short sleeve pattern.

3 From the Contrast fabric, cut:
* One Front Binding
* One Back Binding

Sew on the Neck Bindings

4 Using a stretch or narrow zigzag stitch and a ⅜" (1 cm) seam allowance, sew one long edge of the Front Binding to the right side of the Front along the neck edge. Gently stretch the Neck Binding to fit as you sew. If a small amount of Binding is left at the end of the seam, trim it to match the Front raw edge (**fig. 01**). Repeat to attach the Back Binding to the Back.

5 Press the Front Binding and seam allowances away from the Front, using the iron's steam setting to ease and shape the Binding. Turn the Binding raw edge to the wrong side, over the seam allowances, and press. The Binding raw edge extends just below the seam on the wrong side of the Front and the neckline seam allowances are encased inside the Binding. Pin the Binding in place. Repeat for the Back Binding.

6 From the right side of the Front, sew a zigzag stitch along the bottom edge of the Binding, just above the seam, catching the Binding raw edge on the garment wrong side, finishing the Binding. The rib knit is unlikely to ravel, and the raw-edge finish is more comfortable against the skin than other seam finishes. Repeat entire step to finish the Back Binding.

Sew the Shoulders + Complete the Hems

7 Align the Front and Back at the shoulders, lapping the Back over the Front, matching the shoulder notches and keeping the armhole edges even. Angle and stretch the Bindings slightly to ensure that the entire raw end of each Binding will be caught in the seam and pin the overlapped area in place. Sew zigzag basting seams a scant ⅛" (3 mm) from the raw edges of the shoulders (**fig. 02**).

8 If you have a serger, finish the bottom edges of the Front, Back, and Sleeves. If not, leave the fabric edges unfinished.

9 Press ¾" (2 cm) of the serged (or raw) edges toward the wrong side of the Sleeves. Pin in place if you like—I find it easier to work without pins when stitching crosswise hems.

10 Use a zigzag or other stretch stitch to topstitch ⅝" (1.5 cm) from the folded edge of the Sleeve hems.

Attach the Sleeves + Sew the Side Seams

11 Matching the notch on the Sleeve to the shoulder notches, pin the sleeve to the armhole with right sides together and sew (**fig. 03** on page 126. Work with the sleeve on the bottom, allowing the feed dogs to help ease the curves together. Repeat to attach the remaining sleeve to the other shoulder.

12 With the sleep sack inside out, align and pin the underarm and side seams. Sew one continuous seam,

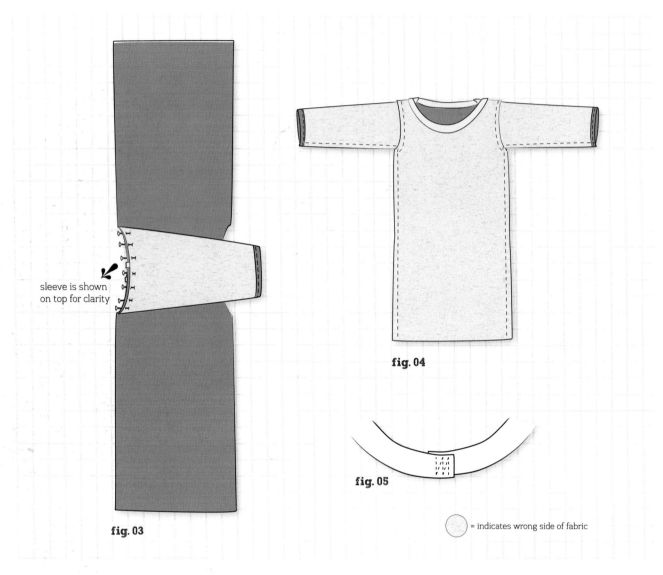

sleeve is shown
on top for clarity

fig. 03

fig. 04

fig. 05

◯ = indicates wrong side of fabric

starting at the sleeve and continuing
to the shirt's bottom edge (**fig. 04**).
Repeat to finish the other side of the
shirt. Press the seam allowances open
if you haven't serged the edges.

13 Press 1" (2.5 cm) to the wrong
side along the bottom edge of
the sack, forming the casing, and pin
if desired. Topstitch with a zigzag or
other stretch stitch ¾" (2 cm) from

the folded edge, leaving a 2" (5 cm)
opening for threading the elastic.

14 Attach a safety pin to one end
of the ½" (1.3 cm) wide elastic
and insert the safety pin into the
casing through the opening. Pin the
other end of the casing to the sleep
sack near the opening, to keep it from
slipping into the casing. Use the safety
pin to work the elastic through the

entire casing and back to the opening.
Remove the safety pin and distribute
the fabric evenly along the elastic.
Overlap the ends of the elastic ½"
(1.3 cm) and stitch together securely
by stitching back and forth a few times
in a zigzag pattern (**fig. 05**). Guide the
join of the elastic into the casing until
it is hidden. Topstitch the opening
in the casing closed, using a zigzag
or other stretch stitch, matching the
previous line of stitches.

A silky-soft kitty can be a much-loved bed-time companion throughout early childhood. Growing up, I had two bunnies that kept me company through nights and naps, bumps and bruises, and playtime. Now they are threadbare and beyond patching, so I made my son his own lovey, sewing much mama-love into each stitch. The kitty also happens to be a puppet, offering little hands the chance to bring their companion to life!

FINISHED SIZE 14½" × 9½" (37 × 24 cm).

FABRIC + MATERIALS

All fabrics should be at least 54" (137 cm) wide

- ⬛ ⅜ yd (34.5 cm) of cotton fleece (Main; *shown:* hemp/organic cotton fleece from NearSea Naturals [see Resources on page 158])

- ⬛ ½ yd (46 cm) of charmeuse for binding, ears, and cheeks (Contrast 1; *shown:* silk/hemp charmeuse in espresso from NearSea Naturals)

- ⬛ ⅜ yd (34.5 cm) of charmeuse for outer body (Contrast 2; *shown:* silk/hemp charmeuse in sand from NearSea Naturals)

- ⬛ Small scraps of wool felt for eyes and nose (*shown:* green and pink)

- ⬛ Cotton embroidery thread to match wool felt

- ⬛ Small amount of stuffing (wool batting is nice) for paws

- ⬛ Sewing threads to match Main and Contrast 1 fabrics

- ⬛ Swedish tracing paper or other pattern paper

TOOLS

- ⬛ Kitty Lovey pattern in pattern envelope

- ⬛ Handsewing needle

- ⬛ Rotary cutter, quilter's ruler, and self-healing mat (optional for cutting)

- ⬛ Silk pins

notes

- ¼" (6 mm) seam allowances are used unless otherwise noted.

- Use the shiny side of the charmeuse and the fuzzy side of the fleece as the right sides.

- Be sure to wash Kitty by hand to preserve the fabric. Why not have your child give it a bath in warm water with a gentle handwashing soap? Kitty will also appreciate lying on a blanket to catch some rays while air-drying, although a shady spot will reduce the chance of fading.

Cut Fabric
+ Make Bias Binding

1 Trace the pattern pieces and Eye and Nose templates onto Swedish tracing paper or other pattern paper, transferring all pattern markings, and cut out.

2 Fold the Main fabric in half lengthwise, with right sides together, and cut the following pieces:
- ✱ One Body on the fold
- ✱ Two Heads
- ✱ Two Arms (cut 1, cut 1 reverse)
- ✱ Two Ears
- ✱ Four Paws

3 From Contrast 1 fabric, cut:
- ✱ Three bias strips: 4⅛" × 18" (10.5 × 46 cm; see page 144 for assistance with cutting bias strips)
- ✱ Two Ears
- ✱ Two Cheeks

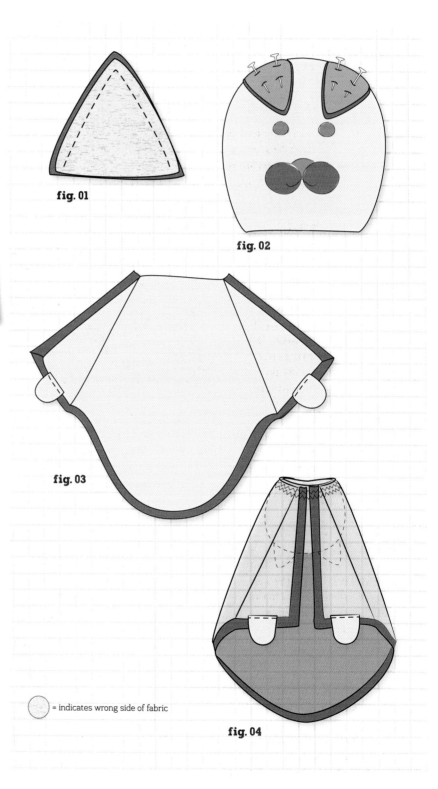

fig. 01

fig. 02

fig. 03

= indicates wrong side of fabric

fig. 04

4 Fold Contrast 2 fabric in half lengthwise, with right sides together, and cut the following pieces:
* One Body on the fold
* Two Arms (cut 1, cut 1 reverse)

5 Use the Eye and Nose templates to cut out two Eyes and a Nose from the wool felt scraps. I find it helpful to use small embroidery scissors while making such small cuts.

Make the Kitty's Head

6 Arrange the Eyes, Nose, and Cheeks on the right (fuzzy) side of one Head piece. Once you've found an arrangement you like, mark each location by making a small dot with a fabric marking pen on the fleece behind each Eye and the Nose. The little nose looks best with its pointy end nestled between the cheeks; refer to the photograph at right for placement. Pin the Cheeks in place.

7 With your machine set to a zigzag stitch 1.4 mm long and 1.6 mm wide, appliqué the Cheeks to the Head, positioning the zigzag stitches to enclose the Cheek raw edges.

8 Attach the Nose and the Eyes to the Head with a whipstitch (page 143), using three strands of matching cotton embroidery floss. Hide the beginning knot between the felt and the fleece, then bring the needle up from the back of the felt to start the whipstitch.

To finish, make a knot on the fleece wrong side, then bury the thread tail between the fabric layers.

9 Use tailor's chalk or a fabric marking pen to draw the mouth, placing it on and between the cheeks, referring

to the photo above and making adjustments as necessary until you are happy with the mouth. Use a backstitch (page 143) and three strands of embroidery floss to embroider the mouth.

10 Place the Contrast 1 Ears right sides together with the Main fabric Ears. Pin and sew, leaving the straight bottom edge open (**fig. 01**). Clip the corners (page 145) and curves (page 145) with embroidery scissors, being careful not to cut too close to the seam. Turn the ears right side out, smoothing the corners into shape, and press flat, using the iron's silk setting (or the appropriate setting for your chosen fabric). Increase the stitch length on your machine and baste the bottom edges of each assembled ear closed, ⅛" (3 mm) from the edges.

11 Place one ear between each set of notches at the top of the embellished Head, with the charmeuse side of the ear against the Head, and pin (**fig. 02**). Lay the second Head on the pinned pieces, right sides together, and pin around the entire curved edge. Sew, using a narrow zigzag stitch (1.0 mm long and 1.4–1.6 mm wide), leaving the straight neck edge open. Clip the curves and turn right side out, smoothing the ears away from the Head. Smooth the curved edges and press the seam. Set the head aside for now.

Assemble + Finish Kitty

12 Place the Main fabric Arms on the Main Body, right sides together, aligning the neck edges and side curves. Pin in place and sew with a narrow zigzag stitch as before. Clip the curves and press the seams open.

13 Repeat Step 12 to attach the Contrast 2 fabric Arms to the Contrast 2 Body, but use a straight stitch in place of the zigzag. Press the seams open. Lay the assembled Contrast 2 Body/Arms on the Main Body/Arms with wrong sides together, matching the raw edges, and pin.

14 Join the Contrast 1 bias strips together to make at least 46" (117 cm) of double-fold bias binding following the instructions under Double-Fold Binding on page 144.

15 Attach the double-fold bias binding to the Body by tucking the Body's raw edges all the way into the center crease of the binding. With the charmeuse layer on top and leaving the neck edge unfinished, pin the binding in place from the neck edge to the first corner.

16 Topstitch (page 142) the binding to the Body a scant ⅛" (3 mm) from the binding's folded edges, stitching through all layers. Check often to ensure that the binding edge on the underside of the project is caught in the stitches as well. Following the instructions under Attaching Binding with Mitered Corners on page 144, miter the corner and continue binding the raw edges all the way to the other side of the neck edge, mitering the remaining corner as instructed. Trim the excess binding even with the neck edge.

17 Place two Paws right sides together and pin. Sew along the curved edge with a narrow zigzag stitch as before, leaving the straight edge open for turning. Clip the curve and turn the Paw right side out, smoothing the curve and pressing lightly. Insert a bit of stuffing into the paw to give it a pillow-like feel. To finish the raw edges, set the machine for a zigzag stitch 1.4 mm long and 4.0 mm wide and overcast the raw edges, closing the paw.

18 Working from the fleece side, pin one Paw to one Arm, positioning it on the curved bottom edge, 1" (2.5 cm) from the corner. Lay the straight edge of the Paw along the binding's inner edge, so the paw hangs free below the binding. Sew through the Paw and binding along the existing binding stitches to attach the Paw (**fig. 03** on page 130). Repeat entire step to attach the second Paw.

19 Find the center of the unfinished neck edge on the Head front and mark with a fabric marker or pin. Wrap the kitty body around the head, with the charmeuse body against the head right side, matching neck raw edges and positioning the bound straight body edges at the head's center front. Pin the neck edges together, matching the Head's side seams to the arm/body seams. The binding's outer edges should meet at the center front but not overlap (see **fig. 04** on page 130).

20 Because the neck opening is small, sew with the inner (wrong) side of the head facing up to facilitate moving the fabric along the feed dogs (you will be sewing with the presser foot inside the neck opening). Use a narrow zigzag stitch to sew around the entire neck seam, beginning where the binding edges abut at the center front. Overlap the stitches at the end of the seam to sew over the bindings twice, reinforcing the most vulnerable part of the seam. Widen and shorten the zigzag stitch and sew the seam allowance edges together, finishing and protecting the seam allowances from raveling with use (**fig. 04** on page 130). Turn the kitty's body right side out and press the seam toward the inside of the head.

tools + materials

There are a multitude of tools and materials available for your sewing projects. Although many of us would love to have every sewing gadget and gizmo out there, most of us need to keep our collections a bit more realistic. This section will give you the breakdown of what you really need to have, as well as outlining some optional materials that are helpful, but not essential.

the essentials

The following are the tools and materials that are essential to have, along with information that will tell you what to look for when buying new equipment.

sewing machine

Although there are some wonderful machines available, featuring a plethora of stitch options, here are some features to look for if you plan to invest in a more modest machine.

Zigzag stitch A machine with the ability to do an adjustable width and length zigzag stitch is a must. Most sewing machines include this as a standard stitch (even very old machines usually have a zigzag stitch function or attachment).

Needle position adjustment capability While not necessary, the ability to adjust your machine's needle so that it sews slightly to the left or right of the center position is a plus.

sewing machine needles ↙

Don't forget to change your machine's needle every two or three projects (or more often as necessary)! Needles come in all shapes and sizes, varying in their sharpness, eye size, and shaft thicknesses. There are also specific needles for sewing on different types of fabrics.

Needle shopping can be confusing, as needle sizes are usually marked with both a European and a U.S. number. U.S. numbers are smaller and on the right (the thinnest needle you can get is an 8) and European numbers are larger and on the left (the thinnest being a 60). Always choose the thinnest needle that has the appropriate point sharpness and eye size for your project (refer to your sewing machine manual or general sewing text for information on choosing a needle for your project).

The next thing to look for is the letter value on the pack of needles. H-M needles have sharper points and are useful for straight and zigzag sewing on both cotton and silk fabrics with either cotton or silk thread. H-E needles are good to use with embroidery thread. If you are stitching on a knit fabric, you'll want to look for a ballpoint needle and/or a stretch needle. Refer to Working with Knits on page 139 for more information.

basic sewing toolkit

The basic sewing toolkit contains the tools and materials that you should have on hand before beginning any of the projects included in this book. Any other tools and/or materials that you need will be listed at the beginning of each individual project.

• Sewing machine and extra needles in a variety of sizes appropriate for the fabrics you are working with (see your sewing machine manual)

• Iron and ironing board (make sure your iron has adjustable temperature settings)

• Straightedge
• Straight pins
• Erasable fabric marking pen or tailor's chalk
• Sewing, craft, and embroidery scissors
• Handsewing needles
• Seam ripper

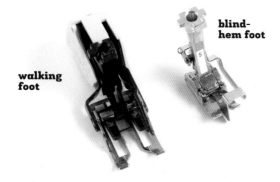

blind-hem foot

walking foot

↑ sewing machine presser feet

Here are some presser feet that will come in very handy for various projects in this book.

Walking Foot: Also called an Even-Feed Foot, it is a great investment if you'll be doing a lot of quilting or sewing on knit fabrics and can also be helpful when sewing binding. It has two sets of "teeth" that grip multiple layers of fabric, minimizing shifting and making it easier to avoid bunching the fabric.

Edgestitch Foot or Blind-Hem Foot: Both of these feet come with a metal "bumper" that glides along the edge of the fabric or appliqué, helping you to make spiffy straight stitches, fret-free blanket stitches, and the blind-hem stitch. One word of caution: a blind-hem foot can do everything an edgestitch foot can, but an edgestitch foot can't do a blind hem.

↓ straightedge

A straightedge is essential for measuring and drawing straight lines. A clear gridded acrylic ruler makes drawing straight lines and squaring corners very easy. You may also want to have a yardstick on hand for marking longer lines. For making straight cuts with a rotary cutter, you'll want to be sure to use a thick, sturdy acrylic ruler, such as a quilter's ruler, as a cutting guide (thinner acrylic rulers, such as the one pictured, are not appropriate for use with a rotary cutter, as they can easily be sliced by the blade).

scissors →

In addition to your sewing scissors, you'll also need a pair of sharp embroidery scissors for clipping around edges and trimming threads, as well as a pair of craft scissors for cutting paper and other non-fabric materials (the latter can simply be an inexpensive pair of standard scissors).

handsewing + embroidery needles

There are a variety of handsewing needles available. Pick the needle that feels the best to you. Generally, the smaller the needle, the less conspicuous the stitch it makes, but the needle must be hefty enough to open a hole in the fabric large enough for the thread. With this in mind, choose a needle that feels sturdy enough that you can handsew with confidence, but also makes the smallest hole possible. I'd start off with a handful of each of the following needle types: Betweens (the shortest), Sharps (slightly longer), and also embroidery or crewel needles (for hand embroidery).

fine ballpoint pins

For working with knit fabrics, you'll want to invest in fine ballpoint pins. The shape of the pins is specifically suited to working with knit fabrics and will not snag or punch holes in the fabric. For working with most woven fabrics, quality straight pins (glass head recommended) are appropriate.

**sewing scissors/
fabric shears**

**embroidery
scissors**

rotary cutter + self-healing mat ↓

Rotary cutters are available in a variety of sizes and feature a sharp rolling blade that makes cutting fabric a snap, especially when cutting multiple pieces and simple shapes, even through several fabric layers. Use a self-healing mat underneath your fabric to protect both your work surface and cutting blade. Although it might take a bit of practice at first, I'm sure you'll soon find yourself wondering how you ever survived without them.

seam/sleeve roll

This is one of those things that I passed by so many times at the fabric store, but now I don't know how I managed without one. When you're sewing children's clothing and other small pieces (such as cuffs), you just insert this long narrow form under the seam to be pressed and press as usual. In conjunction with a steam iron, the roll helps shape pieces, and it can be inserted into sleeves and pant legs to prevent creases in the underlayer.

the extras

Although these tools are not absolutely essential, they are handy to have around.

serger

A serger is a specialized sewing machine that uses multiple threads to finish raw edges with an overlock stitch, while simultaneously sewing the seam and trimming the edge. Sergers are also very helpful (but not essential) for sewing on knits and creating rolled hems. Some sergers are available with a coverstitch option (though these machines are usually more expensive), which is often used on knit garments (for more information on sergers and using one to sew on knit fabrics, see page 140).

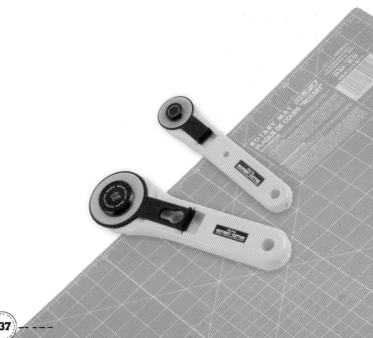

working with knits

For sewing knit children's clothing, you'll need a few extra tricks up your sleeve. In this section, you'll find my recommendations for working with knits, as well as a short primer on the types of knit fabric used in this book.

Types of Knit Fabrics

Three types of knit fabric are used in the projects in this book. In some cases they may be interchangeable, but for other projects the correct choice will make or break the project.

Jersey or T-shirt knits are lightweight single-faced knits. A close look reveals a right side with evenly spaced interlocking loops just like the knit side of a handknit project. The fabric also has a definite wrong side with closely spaced bars of yarn, like the purl side of handknits. Jersey will curl at the cut edges. It is a great choice for lightweight shirts or for reversible projects with two fabric layers back to back. Jersey has enough crosswise stretch to be used in place of ribbing in some projects.

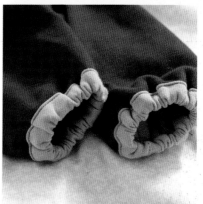

Interlock knits are double-faced and appear the same on both right and wrong sides, so the surfaces can be used interchangeably. Interlock is sturdier and a bit heavier than jersey and doesn't curl when cut. Use interlock for pants and outerwear or in any project where more body is desired. If the interlock has plenty of stretch, it may be used as trim, but its greater bulk makes it less flexible than jersey.

Ribbed knits (or ribbing) have a lot of crosswise stretch and great recovery. That means ribbing will return to its original size quickly and completely after stretching. It is this recovery that allows ribbing to pull a project's body fabric into gentle gathers at a cuff or waistband. When ribbing is applied with very little stretch, it eases around curves just as bias binding would. Rib knits are used to make close-fitting garments and as edge finishes or trim on garments cut from other fabrics.

Choosing + Sourcing Knits for Children's Wear

When choosing a knit fabric for making children's clothing, try to stick with natural fibers in a T-shirt or sweatshirt weight—fabrics that have a good amount of stretch in both directions will be the most comfortable options. For a low-cost source of jersey (T-shirt) and interlock (sweatshirt) knits, look no farther than the thrift store! Pick up men's XL tees and sweatshirts made of 100% cotton, wash them well, and add them to your stash. I'm also partial to some of the organic interlock knit that is sold by individual designers through spoonflower.com. Anybody can draw a design and have it printed through Spoonflower! It's a great source for unique prints. Other sources for jersey and interlock are nearseanaturals.com and banberryplace.com.

Tips for Working With Knits on a Sewing Machine or a Serger

You don't need to have a serger to successfully sew with knit fabrics, although some people prefer to work with a serger if one is available. In fact, with the exception of a few easy straight seams, all of the knit projects in this book were sewn on my regular sewing machine. Many people think that knit fabrics are scary when, in fact, they're pretty forgiving. **Here are some of my favorite tricks for working with knits on a sewing machine and/or a serger:**

• *Know your sewing machine or serger inside and out.* You don't need a serger to sew knits successfully, but you do need to know the capabilities of your machine. Any tips that you read online or pick up in a book won't tell you what settings your machine needs in order to sew knits without frustration. Read the manual and set aside an afternoon to really master your machine, fiddling around with different settings and plenty of scrap fabric. If you purchased your machine (or serger) from a dealer, they usually offer free machine mastery classes for their customers. Find a local dealer (even if you didn't buy your machine from them) and ask about any classes and/or services they have available.

• *Get the right needles for the job.* More often than not, I use Schmetz Stretch needles (130/705 H-S 75/11 or 90/14) for sewing with knits. On heavier-weight knits, I might use a ballpoint/jersey needle, but if I'm getting skipped stitches, I'll switch back to my trusty stretch needle. You'll also want to have Stretch Twin needles on hand for sewing hems and a mock coverstitch (more on this on page 141!).

• *Overlock or zigzag stitch all seams.* Knit patterns are cut with less ease because the fabrics themselves are stretchy, so the seams that you sew on a knit need to stretch as well, or else the thread will break. An overlock stitch on a serger creates a very stretchy and strong seam and is perfectly suited for sewing seams on knits; it will also control the curl of jersey knits. If you're sewing on a regular machine, check your manual to see if it has a mock overlock stitch or a jersey stitch. Both are well-suited for knits. The standard option for sewing seams on a basic sewing machine is to use a zigzag stitch, set to a width of .7 mm and a length of 3.0 mm.

• *Reduce the pressure of the presser foot if your seams stretch as you sew.* If you're getting stretched, wavy seams, it's likely due to too much presser foot pressure. Most machines (and sergers) have the option to change the pressure of the foot; check your manual. If you have a serger and you're getting wavy seams, make sure your differential feed is on the correct setting for knits (refer to your serger manual).

• *Consider using a walking foot.* If you've reduced the pressure of the foot on your regular sewing machine and you're still getting unsightly seams, try a walking foot. This nifty foot grabs both the top and bottom fabrics and feeds the fabric more evenly.

• *Use quality thread and pick up some woolly nylon.* If you plan to use a serger, be aware that sewing the seams will use considerably more thread than a zigzag stitch on a standard sewing machine. Most sergers are also somewhat picky about thread—stick to quality cones of serger thread, such as those made by Mettler, and you'll save yourself a lot of frustration.

Woolly nylon thread is both soft and strong, as well as being stretchy, making it well-suited to sewing knits (although the color choice may be limited). Woolly nylon should generally only be used in the bobbin of your sewing machine or the loopers of your serger. If you use woolly nylon in your serger, make sure to test your settings on a scrap piece of the same type of fabric you'll be sewing. You'll most likely have to adjust the tension of the needle and looper threads. Once I find the setting that works perfectly for woolly nylon on any given knit fabric, I write down the settings on a piece of paper and keep it posted near my serger. This cuts down on the guesswork the next time I use that fabric for a project.

• *Know how to make a professional-looking hem using either a serger or your regular sewing machine.* Even if you're lucky enough to have a serger, you may not have a coverstitch function (if you have this function, learn to use it and practice on scraps before using it on your knitwear). A coverstitch is comprised of the two parallel lines of stitching that you see on the hem of your T-shirts; the wrong side features a looping stitch. The coverstitch is stretchy and creates a very professional finish when it comes to knitwear. If you don't have the option of using a coverstitch, you can still make a professional-looking hem on your sewing machine. See techniques below for instructions on using your sewing machine for hemming knits.

techniques

Here I've included instructions on a few helpful techniques for sewing knitwear.

Hemming Knits with a Sewing Machine

You'll need:
- A sewing machine with twin needle capability (most machines have this)
- a stretch twin needle in either 2.0 or 4.0 mm width
- woolly nylon thread
- fusible web tape, ½" (1.3 cm) wide (optional; recommended: Steam-a-Seam)

1 Press a ⅝" (1.5 cm) hem to the wrong side and pin or baste.

2 Hand-wind a bobbin with woolly nylon thread, taking care not to stretch the thread as you wind, and insert your bobbin into the sewing machine. A mock coverstitch isn't quite as stretchy as a real coverstitch, but the woolly nylon will create extra give in your hem, assuring that threads won't snap during everyday wear and tear.

3 Replace the regular stretch needle with a stretch twin needle. Refer to the sewing machine manual for machine-specific instructions on threading and using a twin needle. Set up the machine, then test the stitch on a fabric scrap. If the fabric tunnels (forms a ridge between the two lines of stitching), reduce the needle thread tension (for example, from a 4 setting to 1). Stitch the hem from the right side, ½" (1.3 cm) from the fold, with the twin needle about ⅛" (3 mm) from the raw edge of the hem.

Optional: Following the manufacturer's instructions, fuse the fusible web tape to the wrong side of the fabric, ⅛" (3 mm) from the raw edge to be hemmed. Remove the paper backing and press the hem, fusing the hem allowance to the garment. Stitch as directed above. **Note** Choose a stitchable fusible web and test it on a scrap to be sure it will not stiffen

the hem unattractively.

Attaching Ribbing to an Edge

1 Cut a strip of ribbing as directed in the individual project instructions, with the crosswise grain parallel to the strip's long edge to take advantage of the fabric's greatest stretch.

2 Lay the prepared fabric piece on a flat surface. Grasp the ribbing at each end and pull, stretching firmly but gently. Lay the ribbing on the work surface and allow it to relax for a moment; it won't completely regain its original dimensions.

3 Lay the prepared ribbing on the fabric, right sides together and raw edges matched, aligning one end of the ribbing with one end of the fabric seamline. Without stretching the ribbing further, ease it into place along the fabric edge and pin.

4 Sew the ribbing to the fabric as directed in the instructions. Trim any excess length from the ribbing. The stretch-and-relax process before sewing the seam will put just enough ease into the ribbing for a smooth attachment without puckers or ripples.

When the ribbing is intended to gather the attached fabric, as on the puffed sleeves of the alternate Crossover Tee (page 25), do not pre-stretch the ribbing. Instead, cut the ribbing smaller than the fabric edge and stretch the ribbing as it is sewn to the fabric. Pin the ribbing at each end to keep it squarely against the fabric's side edges, and place an additional pin at the center to keep the center points aligned.

If interlock knit is substituted for ribbing, cut the strip of interlock knit the same length as the fabric edge to which it will be attached and apply the knit strip without stretching. Use caution when substituting interlock knit for ribbing, remembering that it will stretch considerably less than a same-length strip of ribbing.

terms

BACKTACK Sewing backward over previous machine stitching to secure it in place. This is usually done at the beginning and end of a stitch line. Most sewing machines have a back-tack function; refer to your sewing machine manual for assistance with the settings on your machine.

BASTE Use long running/straight stitches to temporarily secure a seam or other feature in place by hand or machine. The longer length makes the stitches easier to remove when they are no longer needed. To machine-baste, set your machine to a long stitch length; to hand-baste, use long running stitches, spaced about ¼" (6 mm) apart.

EASE/EASE IN Generally refers to sewing a longer piece of fabric to a shorter piece or a curved piece to a straight piece (or two curved pieces). This creates shape in a garment or object without pleats or gathers. To ease pieces together, pin the ends or notches together evenly (or pin as instructed by the pattern), then pin the pieces together at the center or indicated notch(es). Continue pinning the remaining fabric together, allowing the fabric to bubble evenly as you pin, but making sure that the seamlines match up as smoothly as possible (you will be smoothing the excess fabric away from the edge). Stitch slowly, smoothing as necessary to avoid catching tucks in the seam.

EDGESTITCH A line of machine stitching that is placed very close to an edge or exisiting seamline, usually no more than 1/16–1/8" (2–3 mm) away.

FINGER PRESS Pressing a crease or fold by pushing firmly with your fingers instead of using an iron.

GRAINLINE A line marked on a pattern that is used to line up the pattern with the straight grain of a fabric.

LINING Material used to hide the wrong side of a garment or project (and also protect the seams from wear and tear). Usually the lining is a mirror image of the shell.

NAP Fabric texture created by the weave (such as the "ribbing" in corduroy) or a directional print; a fabric with nap necessitates that pattern pieces be placed so that they are oriented in the same direction.

NOTCH A pattern marking placed on the edge to indicate placement of an adjoining piece or other feature. Notches appear as small triangles against the edge of the pattern, with the point of the triangle facing in toward the pattern (see the Pattern Guide on page 146).

OVERLOCK STITCH A stitch used to finish the raw edges of fabric to prevent raveling; it can be produced with a serger. The zigzag stitch on a conventional sewing machine can be used as an alternative to finish the edges.

RAW EDGE The cut edge of the fabric that has not yet been finished by seaming or hemming.

RIGHT SIDE The right side of the fabric is the front side or the side that should be on the outside of a finished garment or project. On a print fabric, the print will be more visible on the right side of the fabric.

RIGHT SIDES TOGETHER When instructed to place pieces "right sides together" the right sides of the fabric should be facing each other.

RUNNING STITCH This basic hand-stitch is made up of evenly spaced stitches and can vary in length according to the intended use or as desired. Running stitches are used for decorative purposes and/or for joining pieces by hand in some cases. See also Straight stitch.

SATIN STITCH (MACHINE) This is a smooth, completely filled column of zigzag stitches achieved by setting the stitch length to 0.2–0.4 mm. The length setting should be short enough for complete coverage but long enough to prevent bunching and thread buildup.

SEAM ALLOWANCE The fabric between the raw edge and the seam.

SELVEDGE The tightly woven borders on the lengthwise edges of he fabric that are created by the weaving or knitting process.

SHELL The material on the outside of a garment or project.

STAYSTITCH A line of stitching made through a single layer of fabric, used to stabilize fabric (preventing distortion). Staystitching is usually placed just inside the seamline.

STITCH IN THE DITCH Stitching directly over a previous seam that has been pressed open or to one side.

STRAIGHT STITCH This basic stitch is the default stitch on your sewing machine and is used for most common sewing applications. This term is also used to refer to a single straight handstitch. See also Running stitch.

TOPSTITCH Stitching that is visible on the outside of a garment or project that is used to provide extra stability and/or for decorative purposes.

WRONG SIDE The underside of the fabric or the side that will be on the inside of a finished garment or project. On a print fabric, the print will be less visible on the wrong side of the fabric.

stitches + techniques

* backstitch

Working from right to left, bring the needle up at **1** and insert behind your starting point at **2**. Bring the needle up at **3**. Repeat by inserting at **1** and then bring the needle up one stitch length beyond **3**.

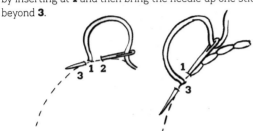

* blindstitch

Take a small stitch in one fabric at **1** (picking up only a few threads), then take the next stitch about ⅛"–¼" (3–6 mm) farther along in the other fabric at **2**, creating a diagonal stitch; repeat until the seam is finished.

* running stitch

Working from right to left, bring the needle up and insert at **1**, ⅛"–¼" (3–6 mm; or longer as necessary) from the starting point. Bring the needle up at **2** , ⅛"–¼" (3–6 mm; or longer as necessary) to the left of **1**, and repeat.

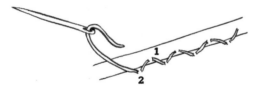

* satin stitch

Satin stitch is most often used to fill in a shape or create a thick scallop-like edge. Bring the needle up at **1**, insert at **2**, and bring back up at **3**. Repeat.

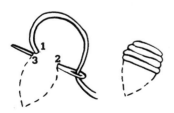

* slip stitch

Take a stitch about ¹⁄₁₆"–¼" (2–4 mm) long into the folded edge of one piece of fabric and then bring the needle out. Insert the needle into the folded edge of the opposite piece of fabric, directly across from the exit point of the thread in the previous stitch. Repeat by inserting the needle into the first piece of fabric as before. This will create small, almost invisible stitches.

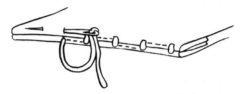

* stem stitch

Working from left to right, bring the needle up at **1** and insert it ⅛"–¼" (3–6 mm) away at **2** (do not pull taut). Bring the needle up halfway between **1** and **3**, at **3**. Keeping the needle above the loop just created, pull the stitch taut. Repeat by inserting the needle ⅛"–¼" (3–6 mm) to the right and bring up at **2**.

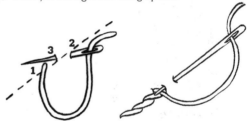

* square knot

Working with two cords (or threads), make a loop from the right cord (pinch the cords together at the base of the loop between thumb and forefinger),  then thread the left cord through the loop from bottom to top. Bring the left cord toward you and wrap it under and around the base of the right loop and then thread it through the loop from top to bottom. Pull the cords tight.

* whipstitch

Bring the needle up at **1** and insert at **2**, then bring up at **3**. The stitches can be as close together or as far apart as necessary.

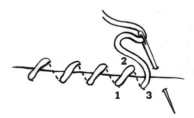

✳ double-fold binding

Cut the fabric strip(s) as directed by the pattern and then follow the instructions under Bias Binding below. Cut a strip long enough to bind the project edge or cut multiple strips and join them end to end according to the instructions under Diagonal Seams for Joining Strips below. Be sure to remove the selvedges (page 142) from the strips.

DIAGONAL SEAMS FOR JOINING STRIPS

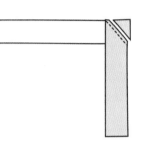

Lay two strips, right sides together, at right angles. The area where the strips overlap forms a square. Sew diagonally across the square as shown at right. Trim the excess fabric, ¼" (6 mm) from the seamline and press the seam allowances open. Repeat to join all the strips, forming one long fabric band.

BIAS BINDING

1. Fold one cut end of the fabric to meet one selvedge, forming a fold at a 45-degree angle to the selvedge (**fig. 01**). With the fabric placed on a self-healing mat, cut off the fold with a rotary cutter, using a straightedge as a guide to make a straight cut. With the straightedge and rotary cutter, cut strips to the appropriate width (**fig. 02**).

2. Fold the strip in half lengthwise, with wrong sides together, allowing one raw edge to extend just past the other edge (about ¹⁄₁₆" [2 mm]), rather than folding it exactly in half; press. The slightly extended edge will make it easier to catch the bottom edge of the finished binding when it is sewn into place around the edge of a project.

3. Open up the fold and then fold each long edge toward the wrong side, so that the raw edges meet in the middle (**fig. 03**).

4. Refold the binding along the existing center crease, enclosing the raw edges (**fig. 04**), and press again.

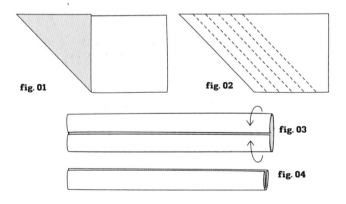

fig. 01

fig. 02

fig. 03

fig. 04

ATTACHING BINDING WITH MITERED CORNERS

1. Place the binding around the edge of the project, snugging the raw edge of the project up into the center crease of the binding (see **fig. 01**). Be sure to place the slightly extended side of the binding on the bottom of the project (see Step 2 under Double-Fold Binding at left). Pin the binding in place to the first corner.

2. Using your walking foot (optional), edgestitch (page 142) the binding to the project a scant ⅛" (3 mm) from the binding's inner edges, stitching through all layers. As you sew along, check often to make sure that you are catching the edge of the binding underneath the project as well. Continue sewing all the way to the first corner and backtack (page 142). Remove the project from the machine and trim the threads (**fig. 01**).

3. From the first corner, fold the binding back on itself (the binding will turn inside out and begin to wrap around the already-sewn binding). On both front and back, crease the binding diagonally into the corner (**fig. 02**), as you fold the binding back down, encase the adjoining raw edge (turning the binding right side out again) and pin in place (see **fig. 03**).

4. Finger press the resulting diagonal fold (miter) at the corner (**fig. 03**).

5. Repeat Steps 2–4 to bind the remaining edges and miter the corners.

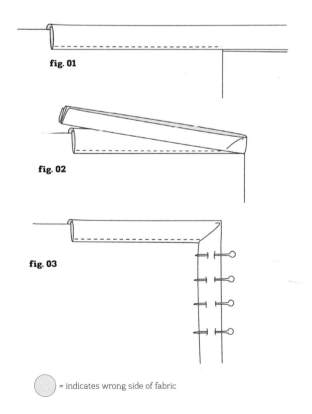

fig. 01

fig. 02

fig. 03

⬤ = indicates wrong side of fabric

* clip the corners

Clipping the corners of a project reduces bulk and allows for crisper corners in the finished product. To clip a corner, cut off a triangle-shaped piece of fabric across the seam allowances at the corner. Cut close to the seamline but be careful not to cut through the stitches.

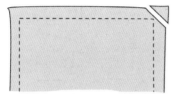

* clip the curves

Clipping the seam allowances along curved edges (concave or convex) reduces bulk and allows the seam to lie flat, eliminating puckering at the seamline. To clip convex curves, make small V-shaped cuts into the seam allowances along the curve; for concave curves, cutting slits will suffice. Cut close to the seamline but be careful not to cut through the stitches. Tighter curves will require more clipping, with the cuts spaced closer together than gentler curves.

* squaring up

When you are creating a quilted project with a layer of batting between the top and bottom layers, you will need to ensure that all layers are flush around the edges before you finish the edges (usually with binding).

Place your project onto a self-healing mat and square up the edges by using a metal yardstick or a rigid clear acrylic ruler (such as a quilter's ruler) and rotary cutter to trim each edge as necessary so that all layers are even and the corners form neat right angles. Use the edge of the ruler as a guide to make straight cuts with the rotary cutter.

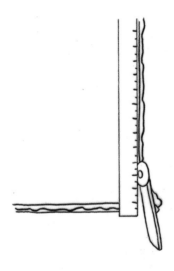

size chart

Newborn to 24 months

SIZE	NEWBORN	3 MONTHS	6 MONTHS	9 MONTHS	12 MONTHS	18 MONTHS	24 MONTHS
HEIGHT	22" (56 cm)	24" (61 cm)	27" (68.5 cm)	29" (73.5 cm)	30½" (77.5 cm)	33" (84 cm)	35½" (90 cm)
CHEST	16" (40.5 cm)	17" (43 cm)	18" (45.5 cm)	18½" (47 cm)	19" (48.5 cm)	19¾" (50 cm)	20½" (52 cm)
WAIST	16½" (42 cm)	17½" (44.5 cm)	18½" (47 cm)	19" (48.5 cm)	19½" (49.5 cm)	20¼" (51.5 cm)	21" (53.5 cm)
HIP/SEAT	16½" (42 cm)	17½" (44.5 cm)	18½" (47 cm)	19" (48.5 cm)	19½" (49.5 cm)	20¼" (51.5 cm)	21" (53.5 cm)

2T to 5

SIZE	2T	3T	4T	5
CHEST	20½" (52 cm)	21" (53.5 cm)	22" (56 cm)	23" (58.5 cm)
WAIST	21" (53.5 cm)	21½" (54.5 cm)	22" (56 cm)	22½" (57 cm)
HIP	21" (53.5 cm)	22" (56 cm)	23" (58.5 cm)	24" (61 cm)

pattern guide

Here is a quick reference guide to the symbols and markings on the patterns, as well as brief instructions on using patterns.

Although you can simply cut the patterns directly from the insert pages, you'll probably want to leave them intact because some of the patterns overlap each other. Instead, trace the selected pattern onto Swedish tracing paper (see Resources on page 158) or other pattern paper (such as butcher paper or newsprint) and cut out. Then you can either pin (not appropriate for all fabrics) the pattern pieces to the fabric and cut around them or weight the pattern pieces in place and trace them onto the fabric with a fabric marking pen or tailor's chalk and then cut out along the traced lines. Be sure to transfer the pattern pieces and all pattern markings to the wrong side of the fabric unless otherwise noted. The exception to this is that placement dots, for things such as pockets, should usually be transferred to the right side of the fabric with a removable marking tool.

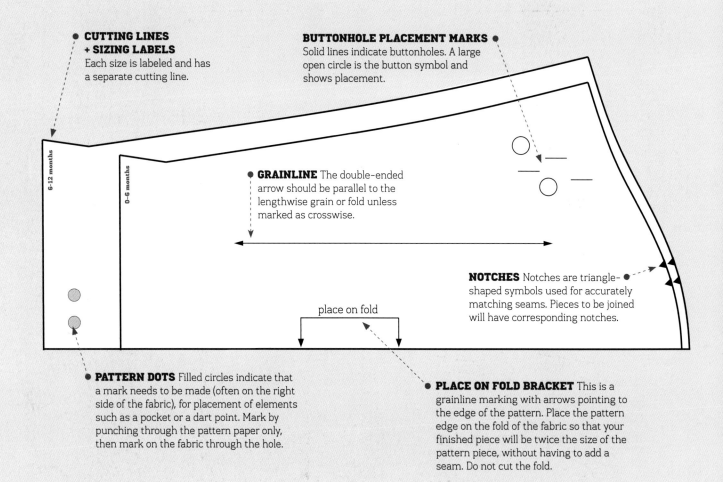

CUTTING LINES + SIZING LABELS
Each size is labeled and has a separate cutting line.

BUTTONHOLE PLACEMENT MARKS
Solid lines indicate buttonholes. A large open circle is the button symbol and shows placement.

GRAINLINE The double-ended arrow should be parallel to the lengthwise grain or fold unless marked as crosswise.

NOTCHES Notches are triangle-shaped symbols used for accurately matching seams. Pieces to be joined will have corresponding notches.

6-12 months

0-6 months

place on fold

PATTERN DOTS Filled circles indicate that a mark needs to be made (often on the right side of the fabric), for placement of elements such as a pocket or a dart point. Mark by punching through the pattern paper only, then mark on the fabric through the hole.

PLACE ON FOLD BRACKET This is a grainline marking with arrows pointing to the edge of the pattern. Place the pattern edge on the fold of the fabric so that your finished piece will be twice the size of the pattern piece, without having to add a seam. Do not cut the fold.

layout diagrams

envelope tees
project shown on page 08

60" (152.5 cm)
All sizes short sleeve

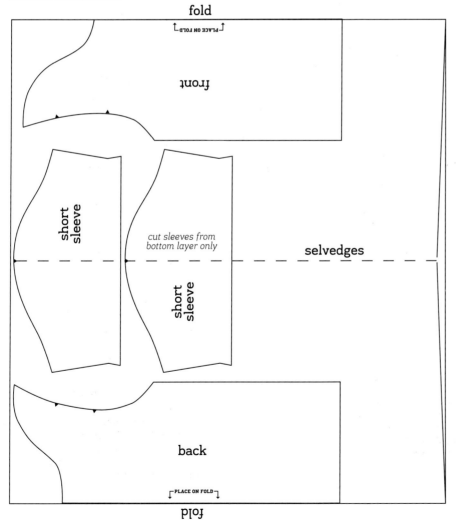

envelope tees
project shown on page 08

60" (152.5 cm)
All sizes long sleeve

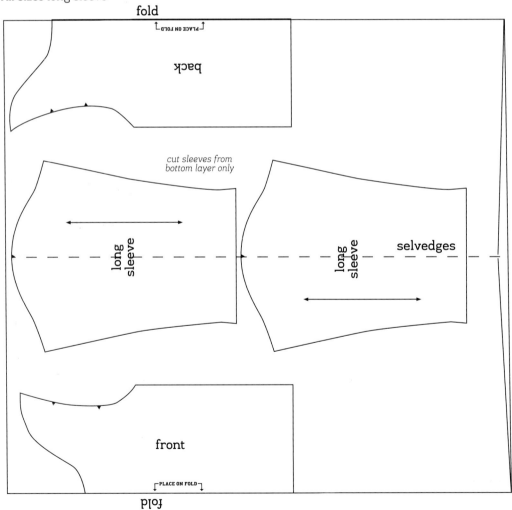

heartwarming reversible baby sweatshirt
project shown on page 12

reversible bubble pants
project shown on page 18

60" (152.5 cm)
All sizes

60" (152.5 cm)
All sizes

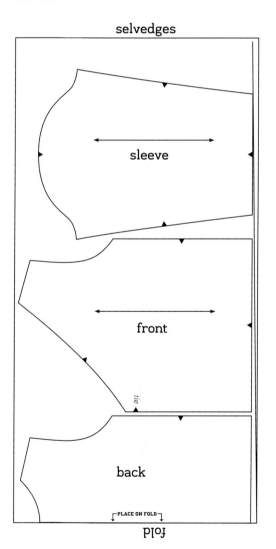

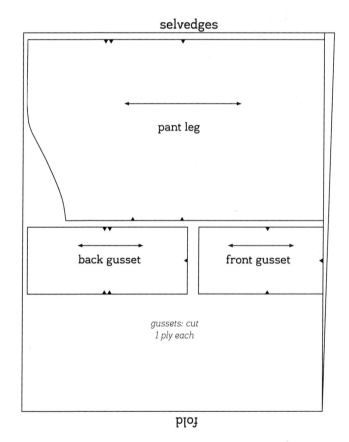

selvedges

sleeve

front

tie

back

⌐PLACE ON FOLD⌐

fold

selvedges

pant leg

back gusset

front gusset

*gussets: cut
1 ply each*

fold

layout diagrams

crossover tees
project shown on page 24

60" (152.5 cm)
All sizes short sleeve

60" (152.5 cm)
All sizes long sleeve

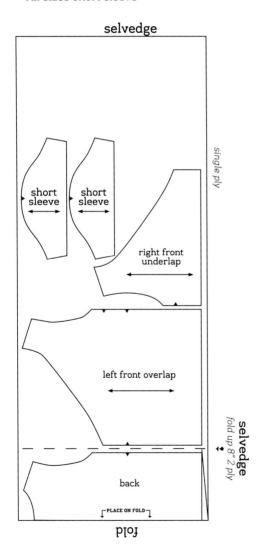

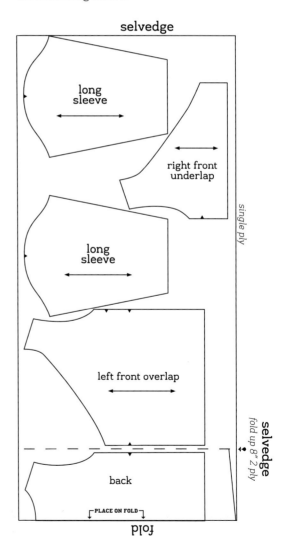

basic pocket pants
project shown on page 30

45" (114.5 cm) Main
2T, 3T

selvedges

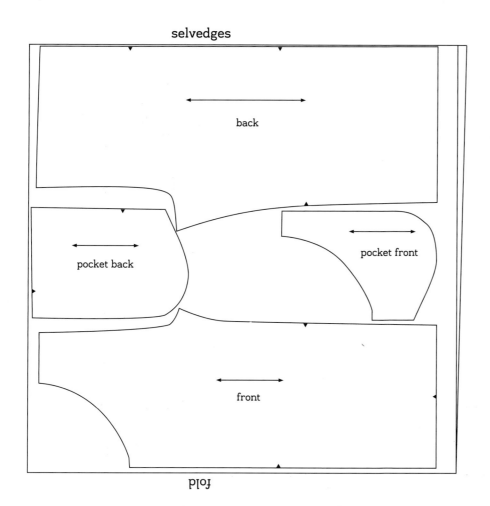

back

pocket back

pocket front

front

fold

basic pocket pants
project shown on page 30

45" (114.5 cm) Main
4T, 5

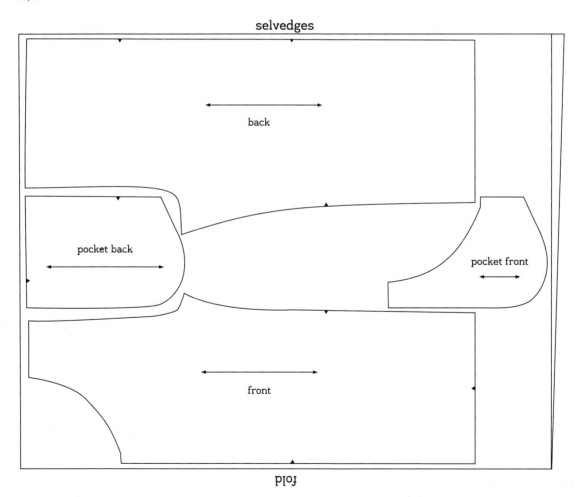

selvedges

back

pocket back

pocket front

front

fold

basic pocket pants
project shown on page 30
58" (shell + contrast)

60" (152.5 cm) Main
All sizes

45" to 60" (114.5 to 152.5 cm)
Contrast

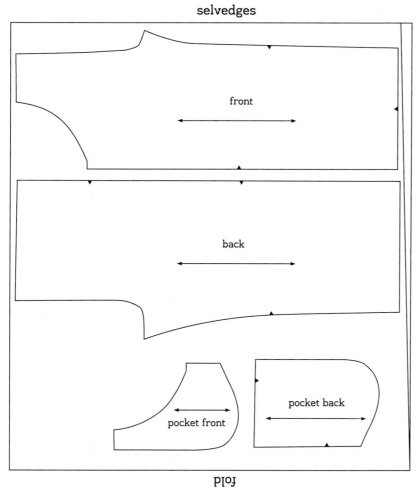

layout diagrams

**reversible hooded
play cape**
project shown on page 80

60" (152.5 cm) Main + contrast
All sizes

selvedges

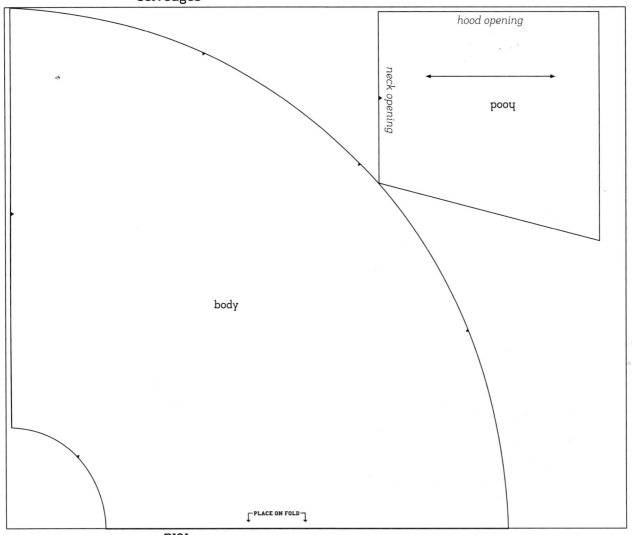

hood opening

neck opening

hood

body

PLACE ON FOLD

fold

hideaway play tent
project shown on page 108

selvedge

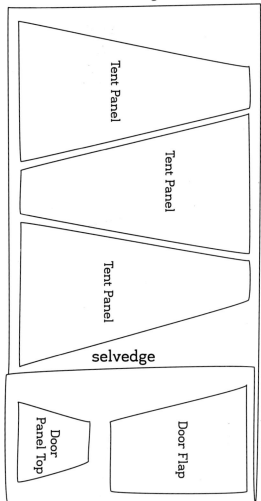

Tent Panel

Tent Panel

Tent Panel

selvedge

Door Panel Top

Door Flap

fold

layout diagrams

sleeping johns
project shown on page 118

selvedges

front/back

fold

baby sleep sack
project shown on page 122

60" (152.5 cm)
All sizes

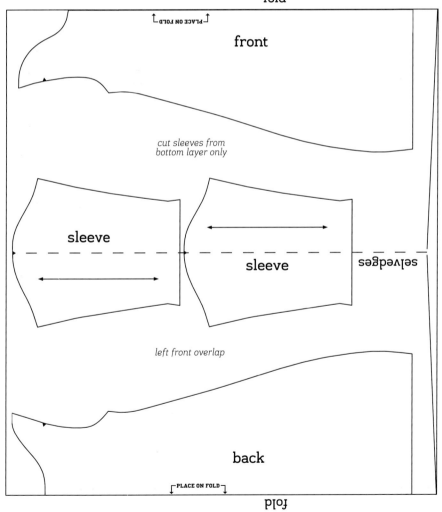

fold

PLACE ON FOLD

front

cut sleeves from
bottom layer only

sleeve

sleeve

selvedges

left front overlap

back

PLACE ON FOLD

fold

resources

Sewing Supplies + Notions

Banberry Place Fabrics
(210) 347-6504
banberryplace.com
Wide selection of knit fabrics, including great striped knits and printed knits for kids clothing

Etsy.com
Wooden tree branch buttons; unique fabrics

Jo-Ann Fabric and Craft Stores
(888) 739-4142
joann.com
Pressing hams; grommets; various sewing supplies; fabric sheets for printer; fabric; and notions

NearSea Naturals
PO Box 345
Rowe, NM 87562
(877) 573-2913
nearseanaturals.com
Swedish tracing paper; organic fabrics, including large selection of knit fabrics; Incandescent Peace Silk; silk/hemp charmeuse

Purl Soho
459 Broome St.
New York, NY 10013
(212) 420-8796
purlsoho.com
Upholstery-weight cottons; quilting cottons; printed knit fabrics; embroidery floss

SlingRings
PO Box 27
Laveen, AZ 85339
(888) 369-3509
slingrings.com
Sling rings

Spoonflower
2810 Meridian Pkwy, Ste. 130
Durham, NC 27713
(919) 321-2949
spoonflower.com
Custom-printed fabric; Wonderfluff fabric featured in All-By-Myself Bib

Doll-Making Books + Supplies

Books
Lang, Hillary. *Wee Wonderfuls.* New York: STC Craft, 2010.
Sealey, Maricristin. *Making Waldorf Dolls.* Gloucestershire: Hawthorne Press, 2005.

Weir Dolls + Crafts
weirdollsandcrafts.com
Doll-making needles; stockinette fabric; flesh-toned knits; yarn for hair; wool batting

Dancing Rain Dolls
http://dancingraindolls.com/Tips_how-tos.html
Crochet doll wig tutorial (my personal favorite method for doll hair)

Art Supplies, Toys + Learning Materials for Children

Blick Art Materials
PO Box 1267
Galesburg, IL 61402
dickblick.com
Caran d'ache crayons; Prismacolor illustration markers; quality paper pads

Blynken and Nod
etsy.com/shop/blynkenandnod
Ready-made nature scavenger hunt cards

Michael Olaf
michaelolaf.com
Blocks; child-size kitchen utensils and cookware

Montessori Services
montessoriservices.com
Learning Tower

Nova Natural
novanatural.com
Simple toys made from wood and other natural material; wooden play kitchens

Paper Source
410 N. Milwaukee Ave.
Chicago, IL 60654
paper-source.com
Mini clothespins

Books + Music

Guthrie, Woody. *Songs to Grow On for Mother and Child.* Smithsonian Folkways, 1992.

Oppenheimer, Sharifa. *Heaven on Earth: A Handbook for Parents of Young Children*, Great Barrington: SteinerBooks, 2006.

Payne, Kim John. *Simplicity Parenting: Using the Extraordinary Power of Less to Raise Calmer, Happier, More Secure Kids*, New York: Ballantine Books, 2010.

Raffi. *The Singable Songs Collection.* Rounder/Umgd, 1996.

Soule, Amanda Blake. *The Creative Family: How to Encourage Imagination and Nurture Family Connections*, Trumpeter Books, 2008.

Inspirational Blogs, Web Sites + Magazines for Parenting + Crafting

sewliberated.typepad.com

themontessorigoldmine.blogspot.com

soulemama.typepad.com

Mothering magazine
mothering.com

Living Crafts magazine
livingcrafts.com

Stitch magazine
interweavestitch.com

index

Get more creative sewing projects
with these inspiring resources from Interweave

Sew Liberated
20 Stylish Projects for
the Modern Sewist

Meg McElwee

ISBN 978-1-59668-161-3
$24.95

49 Sensational Skirts
Creative Embellishment Ideas
for One-of-a-Kind Designs

Alison Willoughby

ISBN 978-1-59668-061-6
$24.95

Sewn
Classic
Clothes

Fiona Be

ISBN 978
$26.95

Make Time to Sew Daily

SewDaily is an online community that is all about
contemporary sewing, all the time, so you can get
a regular dose of sewing inspiration every day. Get
free patterns, read blogs, check out galleries, chat
in forums, and get inspired by your fellow sewists.
You'll also get a free e-newsletter, event updates, tips
and techniques, and more. Sign up at **SewDaily.com**

stitch
CREATING WITH FABRIC + THREAD

Stitch magazine brings you contemporary style
and essential sewing information for both new and
experienced sewing enthusiasts. Whether you make
garments, home décor projects, or accessories, you'll
find a trove of captivating designs, step-by-step
instructions, and well-written articles sure to inspire.
Interweavestitch.com

INTERWEAVE
interweave.com